ELECTION

LOVE BEFORE TIME

Kenneth D. Johns

PRESBYTERIAN AND REFORMED PUBLISHING CO.
Nutley, New Jersey
1977

PRINTED IN THE UNITED STATES OF AMERICA

Table Of Contents

PREFACE

This book is about a word. That word is ELECTION. It will not accomplish all that we need in our personal lives and the church, but it will do much. It will do more for us than we can possibly imagine. It will do no more than we will allow it to do. With study and trust it will open doors of possibility and opportunity, doors we could not have seen or passed through before.

It is not a human word, it is a Divine Word. Given by God for men and women who without it will experience more despair and frenzy in their work for Christ than is needful.

It is a word which speaks to every Christian.

A mother raising children.

A soul-winner.

A preacher laboring in a hard place.

It is a good word.

Give it a chance. It comes from God.

CHAPTER ONE
SOMETHING WRONG HERE!

As the years pass I am becoming increasingly distressed with the manner by which men explain the doctrine of Divine Election. In introducing the subject to many friends and ministers, I have discovered that some simply do not want to talk about it. It has caused them difficulty in the past, possibly because some contrary learner stirred up strife when the idea was being openly and honestly discussed. The minister then felt it was not worth going through the same frustration again to get at this truth. "Why upset a congregation with it, especially since they need the more basic truths anyway?"

There are others who will talk about election but with a preconceived notion that empties the doctrine of all significance. They speak with the weight of much theological thought behind them. Their thoughts are echoes of many past debates. Their answer is this. "Surely God chooses men. From eternity He saw who would believe the Gospel when it was preached to them and He chose them because He saw beforehand that they would accept Him." They readily admit the sovereignty of God. They preach the "free-will" of man. But they sense that there is an inconsistency in the biblical revelation concerning these two truths. So they have made up a compromise. And that is precisely what it is. Not willing to let God be God and to do what He wants to with His own clay, they take away from His sovereignty. They make it subject to man's free-will. Man is exalted to a position where he is capable of choosing God. God is lowered to a position where He is only choosing those who choose Him. He is not the Initiator. He is only the Responder. He moves second. Man moves first.

By following this course of reasoning the Christian has arrived at a supposed truth untaught by the Bible. It is in effect a third concept. The first concept is that God is Sovereign. He is able to do and has a right to do anything He desires with anyone or any material. And in doing so He is not answerable to man or man's idea of justice or fairness. The second concept is that of the responsibility of man. Inherent in the responsibility of man is,

1

of course, the idea of man's free-will. Man is responsible for his actions. His fate is determined by his own personal response to the Gospel. His will is not fettered by Divine decree. He cannot blame God for his sins or poverty of spirit.

The Christian would do well to leave these two truths where the Bible leaves them, separate. Though they represent to our minds contradictions, they are both taught in the Word of God; but the Bible makes no attempt to reconcile them. Why should we? In a book written by the Spirit of God and conveying to man the mind of God, why should there not be paradoxes? But man is not content with the paradoxes. He must reconcile them. He must harmonize the inconsistencies. So he develops a third concept. He melts together the Sovereignty of God and the responsibility of man. Not willing to face the fact that the Bible says that God chooses some men for salvation, apart from a consideration of their faith or good works he compromises the rights of God. He makes God's choice dependent upon man's choice. He takes away from the sovereignty of God and adds to the sovereignty of man. Now his preaching about His God does not have the full force of biblical sovereignty. Nor does his view of man have the truth of the impotency and death of human nature. In seeking to satisfy his human reason, he has arrived at a concept not found in the Word of God. It can only be supplied by human reasoning. It seems to me that that is a supply from which the Bible forbids us to draw. For while it may pacify the mind as it wrestles with its God, it does not submit itself to the Divine Revelation. And as any such answer will do it pollutes the stream of divine grace.

Were it just a matter of words or semantics we could dismiss the debate. But it is more than that. It is a matter of essentials. There is first of all the essential of being honest with the Word of God, of being diligent seekers of truth. Is it honest to consider such scriptures as Romans 9; John 6:44, 65; Acts 13:48; Ephesians 1:4,11; Romans 8:28-31; or John 15:16 and force upon them the notion that they all speak of man's choice determining God's choice? It has never failed to startle me that men who should know better have shunted aside these significant verses by simply remarking "Well, God saw who would believe and then He chose them." To hear its constant repetition you would almost think it was an inspired quotation. But I don't find anything like that in the Bible.

In spite of the fact that it is not in the Word of God, this notion prevails among many Christians. It is the standard rebuttal to anyone seeking honest information about the grand words of Election, Calling, and Predestination. The eager and inquiring mind of the new Christian is sometimes permanently stifled by this thrust of human reason. It sticks in

2

his mind with force. It seems to agree with his logical faculties and therefore it strikes again and again against the biblical but paradoxical doctrine of the Sovereign election of God. Why is this so? Why does the human mind, especially the human mind of the believer seize so strongly upon a notion unrecorded in the Bible?

There may be many answers. I would speak of two. The first pertains to the nervousness of the human psyche. Wanting certainties and assurances it attaches itself tenaciously to plausible answers. It does not like the insecurity of thinking through issues. The instability of "not-knowing" during the research period somehow terrifies the man. And so when someone offers an answer to any dilemma, if it has any attraction to the mind, it is adopted immediately and becomes the standard reply to relevant questions. The logic of the plausible solution overcomes the questions. Now the question is resolved. There is no more nagging. No more wrestling. The question does have a real, biblical, ultimate answer. But the divinely aroused inquiry has been faked out by the humanly supplied logic. The dilemma is quieted by a tranquilizer.

The doctrine of Election sets up just such a dilemma in the mind of the believer. When the subject of Predestination or Election is broached the mind feels a tremor. The concept is repulsive. A vision of an arbitrary and despotic God puts panic in the heart. "It cannot be," he says. "God would not choose without regard to human merit and initiative." This usually takes place early in one's Christian experience. And in the same early moments of Life Eternal the answer is provided. For here comes the wise counsellor. He speaks with the seasoned perspective of one who has calmed many similar troubles. He knows the forthcoming reasoning almost always relieves the sufferer. The prescription is derived from reason. Logic, not the Word, will quiet the heart. It has worked before. Wisdom begins, "God indeed is Sovereign, but man has a free will. He can accept or reject salvation. During his lifetime the Gospel will be offered to him. If he rejects it he is lost. But if he accepts he will be saved. God knows which action he will take because God is omniscient. And since He knows who will accept He has chosen them for heaven. He chooses you when he sees that you will choose him." What more could the inquirer ask? The Sovereignty of God has been granted. The much heralded "free-will" of man has been considered. And very deftly the two have been blended to satisfy the logical section of the brain. Court is adjourned. Wisdom has spoken. The issue settled. And from that point on the young believer counts himself much wiser. He is ready to share with any other novice the "fruits" of "diligent" study and "honest" inquiry. A thousand puzzles have now been solved for

3

him. The worst of which is the fact that for the rest of his Christian life he will not have to take seriously the words Election and Predestination. Whenever they pop up in his reading of the Book his little logical "cuckoo bird" will pop out and say: *"...Man chooses God then God chooses Man...Man chooses God then God chooses Man."* The voice of wisdom has spoken. The mind was temporarily agitated and excited as it felt the promise of a great discovery. But the great discovery would have taken time and some wear and tear on the nervous system. Some readjustment of thinking. Some honest submission to the Word of God. Better to have little trouble and little answers. The heart is satisfied; only the deep inner spirit is still unhealed. For the man has not yet found his God.

The second explanation of the ready acceptance of unproved solutions has special application to the doctrine of unconditional election. The very nature of the teaching of election makes man totally subject to God. Not only does it make man's actions subject to God but it will in the end make the man submit his mind and intellect to God's method of operation without a full explanation. A real understanding of election makes a man stand back and accept the fact that his God really is absolute Lord. He can do what He desires. He will always act in harmony with the perfection of His personality, but those actions will not always be acceptable to man. Man rejects this position of submission. He hates the autocracy of God. His very nature cries out against any force which does not explain its motives and purposes to him. Man feels his own sovereignty is jeopardized by any one, especially God, who can act in a sovereign manner over that man's own destiny. And the man who sees election as the Bible preaches it will feel a lessening of pride and self-reliance which is humbling. Man becomes uncomfortable when faced with the implications of Divine Sovereignty. In the Garden man set out to rule his own world, to have things his own way. The battle of "Who shall rule?" has raged ever since. Now election forces him to accept the fact that he not only cannot govern his own world, but he cannot and did not choose God. He did not just become a believer, God made him a believer. This is quite deadly to man's feeling of self-sufficiency. This is quite terminal to any idea of human goodness. Man finds himself in the dust and he doesn't like it. But that is where God wants him and in the end he will be better off in the dust than standing on the imagined bulwark of his own sovereignty.

O wise counsellor,
What would you say?

If you really knew
That God made the way?

You don't really see it,
Because you are fickle.

You've reduced God's love,
To barely a trickle.

You may be puzzled
To be called such a name.

It's very simple really,
Reason's your game.

You open the Bible
To see what God commands.

Then you amend it
As reason demands.

Next you stand and cry,
"The truth I've found!"

"I've wrestled with God
And brought it down,"

And "down" is more true
Than the "truth" you speak.

For when reason is through,
Truth is bleak.

CHAPTER TWO
THE QUESTION AND THE ANSWER: ROMANS NINE

If the reader has been sufficiently aroused to pursue the issue further, then let him consider the direct teachings of the ninth chapter of Romans. More than any other portion of the Word of God this chapter sets forth the doctrine of unconditional election and answers sufficiently the human objections.

It becomes apparent to the pursuer of truth as he studies the ninth chapter of Romans that the Bible is not afraid of portraying God as He really is: One who chooses those who are to be saved. This choice is unconditional, meaning that He chooses them for no reason to be found in them. He acts according to the counsel of His own will. Man may feel this is not right or fair but apparently the Holy Spirit did not share this feeling. For He caused to be written by Paul the telling words: "Jacob have I loved, Esau have I hated." He also explains to us that his choice was made completely apart from any consideration of works or merit or faith, "For the children being not yet born neither having done any good or evil, that the purpose of God according to election might stand, not of works, but of Him that calleth." The doctrine of God's choice of those who are to be saved is put right out in the open for any one with a Bible to read. No apology or explanation of God's decision is offered. It is only for us to read and believe. If the Word teaches this truth, and it does, then it is ours only to believe it and know that our God was not acting out of alignment with the Divine personality in making the choice of the elect.

But man is not so convinced. He feels embarrassed by the statements of the Holy Spirit. He feels he must rescue God from any possible misunderstanding. So he inserts the extra-biblical idea that God's choice is determined by man's choice. This is supposed to give us a more tolerable view of God. It makes Him more acceptable to man's idea of how God should act. But, of course, this is not exactly what the text is saying, so there must be some adjustments in the text. For after all, we can't hold a view unsupportable from the Bible. Let us consider some of the offerings to help the Holy Spirit explain himself.

The first and most natural move man makes to explain away the apparent injustice of God in unconditional election is to claim that God must have seen something in Jacob which He did not see in Esau. The suggestion is that He chose Jacob because He saw from His eternal viewing platform something in Jacob's future conduct or character which would make him preferable to Esau. Jacob may have had more determination or more humility. He may have been more predisposed to accept God. More thankful. But this is nonsense. For this idea is precisely what the text forbids. Romans 9:11: "For the children, being not yet born, neither having done any good or evil, that the purpose of God according to election might stand, not of works, but of him that calleth." The text states categorically that the choice was made before birth. It was made without regard to human activity, good or bad. It is stated in the Inspired Word that the choice was made without any regard to any foreseen quality. Jacob was chosen for the reason that his choice stood within the divine purpose. The Word simply forbids us to tamper with the thought so clearly and forcibly recorded from the mind of God. Let the implications be what they may, God has spoken.

The unconditional election of Romans 9:11 is so patent that even a hurried reading forces it upon the mind. It cannot be circumvented. But not all are content to leave it there. And so another ploy is attempted. If God did choose Jacob over Esau without consideration of their character as the grounds of His choice, maybe it will help us if we can at least soften God's emotions toward Esau. "Esau have I hated," hardly belongs in the Word. Let it read "Esau have I loved less" or "Esau have I disliked." This would be less objectionable. But this will not help solve the issue of the apparent injustice of God. For whatever adjustments are made in the wording, the inequity must remain in the human mind. For unless you can change the word "hate" into the word "love" you end up with God favoring one man over another. For if God ever made a decision to bless one man over another, even to the smallest degree, then He can be charged with being unfair. (Of course, the thought of charging God with injustice is unthinkable; we speak only as men.) But this would be true even if the inspired record said, "Jacob have I loved much, Esau have I loved little." The degree of injustice would be less, but the injustice remains. God would then not be treating men with exact equity. So the appeal to the precise meaning of "hated" fails to rescue God's character from the humanly intolerable view of apparent divine injustice.

The next method used to escape the implications and patent meaning of these verses is to make them applicable only to the nations which existed in the loins of Jacob and Esau. "Election here is only a national question," it is said. This idea suggests that God was not so much choosing individual man as He was forming nations. And therefore election does not pertain to individual salvation but to national privilege. It would say that no one is chosen to be saved and go to heaven; men are elected only to enjoy privilege of opportunity. From that point men work out their own choices. Some are in a more advantageous position, such as the descendants of Jacob who had the Law and the Prophets. Some are more or less in a handicapped position of being estranged from the central privilege of God's people.

There are two basic problems with this argument. First of all we still do not get rid of the issue of the apparent inequity of God's dealings with man. And secondly the text indicates very clearly that individuals and individual salvation are involved.

The first objection is answered with the same reasoning which showed that there is no point in softening the word "hate" in Romans 9:13. For if God shows any partiality in dealing with nations *or* individuals, then he can be charged with injustice in man's eyes. If Romans Nine is only speaking of the election of nations we have the same problem of unfairness. One nation being elected to be the favorite of God, to receive the Law, the Prophets, the Messiah, the Written Word. This advantage is immense. It cannot be calculated. Paul is aware of the great advantage of the Jew and he states it clearly and emphatically in Romans 3:1, *"What advantage then hath the Jew? Or what profit is there of circumcision? Much every way: Chiefly, because that unto them were committed the oracles of God."*

The Jews possessed an infinite advantage over the Gentiles in the matter of individual salvation. Even without personal election national election makes it veritably certain that those in the chosen nation are more likely to be saved. What of most of us? Born and raised in believing homes. Is that not an advantage over the heathen? Living usually within walking distance from a Bible-believing church. Can you say that of the pagan? A Bible upon the table. Millions of the world do not have that. Apparent inequity? Certainly. But yet it is consistent with the methods of the Sovereign God as we know them from revelation. Laying aside the Sovereignty of God are we to call these things accidents? Are you going to heaven because of the accident of your natural birth? Did you just happen to be born where faith was known or did you arrange it?

I am unimpressed with this argument of national election. And it seems to me most of those who use it are also unimpressed. It just doesn't make sense and it fails to bear conviction, even to the mind of those who adopt it. It is without question that the election of God mentioned in Romans Nine is connected with the establishment of nations. With this promise Genesis agrees *"two nations are in your womb"* (Genesis 25:23). But this does not cancel the issue of individual election. Nor does it eliminate from the essence of the issue individual election.

The second objection to the argument of national election only in Romans Nine is that the text indicates very clearly that individuals and individual salvation are involved. We might start with the thirteenth verse itself: "Jacob have I loved, Essau have I hated." God has focused upon an individual man, Jacob. He has loved him. In the end He will make a nation of him, but in the beginning He has selected and loved an individual. There is here a definite preference of and movement toward one man. And this choice was one in which God made distinction of one man and one nation over another man and another nation. One man and his nation would bear a distinct and inherent place in the redemptive purpose of God. As a result of this choice this man has a considerable advantage in those redemptive plans. That is an understatement. For in his election Jacob was actually placed into redemptive fellowship with God, "Jacob have I loved."

Another consideration is found in verse 16 where the obvious application is of personal salvation.

"So then it is not of him that willeth, nor of him that runneth, but of God that sheweth mercy." What can this mean if it does not refer to individual salvation? Is it talking about "willing" and "running" to start a nation? Who could read this verse and suggest that the essence of it refers only to national destiny? Mercy is a word which speaks of redemption. And Paul's clear testimony is that there is only one way to account for personal salvation, and that is the mercy of God, not human effort, faith, or activity. John Stifler sums up Paul's thought,

> The conclusion follows. God's mercy is not the response to human desire or human effort. It is not of him that "willeth" or wishes it, as Moses did, and not of him who "runneth" in the path of right. Willing and running may indicate the possession of grace, but they are not the originating cause. They may be the channel, but they are not the foundation. The source of Grace is God's own will, that goes out to whom he will. Mercy is "of God, that showeth mercy" independent of any motive in man.

Verse 16 is certainly speaking of individuals and teaches that man's will and faith are not factors in the first and determinative movements of personal salvation.

The issue of individual election is touched upon again in verse 18. It must

9

be of individuals that Paul speaks in this text. The concept becomes vacant if we allow this to speak of nations only. A nation cannot be hardened without its people being hardened. A nation cannot receive mercy without the individuals of that nation receiving a personal application of that mercy. Again, John Stifler says it succinctly,

> The subject is not one about nations, but about individuals, not about ethnic supremacy or leadership, but about personal salvation."

It must be recognized and acknowledged that Paul's purpose in Romans 9-11 is to consider Israel's rejection during New Testament times and to put it into proper perspective. He writes that Israel's rejection is not inconsistent with either God's Word or God's justice. Neither is their rejection final. It is their own fault due to their unbelief, but there will come a time when their eyes will be opened and they will be saved (Rom. 11: 25-29). It is apparent, therefore, that Paul is speaking of the issue of a nation, Israel. But in doing so, it is without question, that he touches in a significant and telling way on the question of the election of men and women to personal salvation. And furthermore, it is obvious that this election is unconditional. There is no other conclusion which can be drawn from the concepts of Romans Nine.

If it is further objected that Paul does not teach that election is completely apart from considerations of man's will and effort then Romans 9:14 will prove to the contrary. The question recorded in verse 14 becomes irrelevant if Paul taught a conditional election in the verses leading up to it. Recall that Paul has stated:

1. that the choice of Jacob was made before the occurrence of any good or evil actions;

2. that the children had not yet been born;

3. that Jacob is loved;

4. that Esau is hated.

All of these statements set up a concept of God's methods which appears unjust to man. Paul is aware of this. And he knows that the people who read his letter will be aware of this. He knows that this is the impression they will receive from his message in verses 1-13 of chapter 9. He knows they will see the implications of the concept and he knows that their minds will be bothered by those implications. So he anticipates the problem and asks the question which he sees will be on their minds: "Is there, then, unrighteousness with God?"

10

With the coming of the question, we have come upon the strategic moment. From this question two conclusive arguments force themselves upon us. The first argument has to do with the necessity of the question. Why did Paul feel the question must be phrased? It is obviously more than a teaching device. He doesn't ask questions for the sake of pointless interrogation. So why does he feel the need of stating an objection to what he has just said? *Because He does indeed teach unconditional election.*

He has stated it explicitly. It is patent in the text of verses 1-13. He knows that those who read will see it as he has written it. And he knows that the logical faculty of their minds will compel the question. Therefore we know that Paul was teaching unconditional election, for the objection would never have been anticipated or phrased if he had taught an election based upon man's choice or effort. The question arises from the fact of unconditional election which he has just set forth. The truth of unconditional election is established by the presence of the question.

The second argument is even more forceful than the first, and also clearer. For now with the presence of the question Paul has arrived at the exact moment when he could clarify his position. If he had felt that he needed to qualify his thoughts of verses 1-13 now is the time to do it. If he had needed to modify the unconditional election of verses 1-13 to present the exact picture of election which was upon his mind then the question of verse 14 provides the opportunity. But what does he do? Does he say, "Now I haven't expressed myself too well. You may have misunderstood me, let me explain"? Does he hedge, "Now I don't want you to get me wrong, election isn't quite the way I have described for you"? Does he rationalize, "Now I know this is difficult for you, but it will all clear up when I get to my 'section' on free-will and God's foreknowledge"? Does he make any attempt to adjust his thoughts to man's idea of justice and fairness? No, not for a moment. Instead, he pushes forward to offer more proof from Scripture that such sovereign activity by God is typical of His dealings in the Old Testament.

He refers to Moses and Pharaoh as examples of God's sovereign decisions. He does not back away from his position for a moment. There are no modifications or qualifications. He offers no mystical or metaphysical explanations such as "God lives in eternity and man lives in time. Therefore man's decisions are always contemporaneous with God's decisions." He doesn't just throw the subject up to speculation concerning the infinity and mystery of God. He marches forward to establish the truth with more force and conclusiveness. He will not back away from it. He knows where he stands. He knows himself too well to see his own

11

conversion as anything but a sovereign act of God. He was "willing" and "running" after the hated Christians when God caught him with "mercy." It can be no other way for Paul. Nor for us.

While he is pushing the argument forward he comes to the question which brings us to our knees, "Nay, but, O man, who art thou that repliest against God? Shall the thing formed say to him that formed it, Why hast thou made me thus?"

He will take no more evidence from history. Now he turns to the very nature of the relationship between God and man. And we turn to man's quietest moment in the Word. In hushed and trembling tones he tells us who we are. He reminds us of who God is. Who are we to say, "Why doth he yet find fault?" Not since the moments of Job's encounter with the Almighty (Job 38-42) has man felt so powerfully the place of his God. Neither here nor there is an explanation offered for the behavior of God. But instead man is shown his place far below the Almighty God. What if God does destine men? It is not our place to object "Who hath resisted his will?" Since when does the clay put the potter on the stand? Since when does the creature interrogate the Creator? Can he even entertain the idea without sinful arrogance?

Angels must hide their faces from the man who would ask the Almighty to justify his actions. Paul says, "O man, be careful. Be quiet. Close your mouth. Stop your mind from these thoughts. Let God be God. You have found Him in these moments, do not use them to quarrel. Take your place. Be the creature. You will find enough wisdom in what has been revealed, do not object to what you cannot understand."

Our beloved friend Paul sees the answer to the difficult issue of election not in making a compromise between the Sovereignty of God and the responsibility of man, but in the staggering difference in spheres between the world of man and his God. The answer is not to be found in the searching of logic. The solution is unreachable by human thought. Let God be God and the truth will trouble you no longer. "Hath not the potter power over the clay, of the same lump to make one vessel unto honor, and another unto dishonor?"

In the answer of Paul to the question of verse 14 we come to the final blow upon human pride. We have reached the low point of man's experience of himself. Once acknowledge this truth, that God chose him and he did not choose God, and men will have to travel down no further. Simple lessons of humility may be forthcoming but they will never bring a surprise. Man has found out what he is.

The path to creaturely humility began when the Gospel was first learned.

"All have sinned and come short of the glory of God" was the first declaration. "Wherein have I sinned" was the self-assured reply. "You have broken the law, the ten commandments. You need to be justified from your ungodliness. You must be justified by faith in the blood of Christ, there is no other hope." Conscious of our external and sometimes inward violations of the law we tremble before its wages and submit to our Saviour. Humble enough to move under the Cross, we feel we have made the right decision. We have decided for Christ. Eternal life is ours because of our decision. How thankful we are that we made it. How humbly thankful we are that made it. And indeed it is a blessed humility. But there is more to come.

The fellowship of the redeemed is sweet. The church offers such fellowship, and holiness is such enjoyment. We are unaware of the approaching conflict. Flesh against Spirit. Spirit against Flesh. We cannot do the things that we would. We are puzzled. What has happened? What is this thing within me? Why is it such a struggle? Certainly not the same with every man, but every man must learn the lesson: "For I know that in my flesh there dwelleth no good thing." The lesson seems to be most often learned after the cross than before. Christian is struggling. He is learning about his heart. His sins pained him before the Cross. Now his heart hurts him. And only the healing presence of the Spirit of Christ brings him relief as he learns to walk by the new presence. The old heart cannot be trusted. He walks lower now, but he is reaching higher. He found out he was dead when he first heard the Gospel; now he learns that he stinks. "Blessed humility, how glad to find thee. I am free. It is so wonderful, why don't others choose you as I did?" A further lesson awaits.

"Prayer, the Fellowship, the Word; all are more and more delightful. I cannot spend enough time in the Book. But as I read a word strikes me. 'Election.' Another word. 'Predestination.' What do they mean?"

Even before the "wise counsellor" (Chapter 1) arrives, the mind suggests that logic can supply the answer. The man says, "It must be that God knew I would choose Him and so He chose me.

"But let me read further. What is that? 'Chosen before the foundation of the world?' Look here. 'And he said, therefore said I unto you, that no man can come unto me, except it were given unto him of my father.' This can't be....'And as many as were ordained to eternal life believed.' What is the meaning of all this? How can it be?

"I thought I chose. I thought my will brought about my birth. Did I not will to be saved? Certainly. But what was behind my will? What moved it? Could it be that I sought Him because he moved me to seek him? Could it be that He put it into my heart to come? Could it be that I am that low? That I was that dead? Could I have fallen that far?"

(Terrible illumination, those moments, but holy ground. A man has found his God. A man has found himself. He knows now who he is. He knows now who his God is. They will not leave each other. They have been friends too long.) "God's mind has held me from eternity. I will love Him for eternity. You have brought me very low, Father, to take me very high. I cannot speak. I will not reply."

His head had once bowed before the Cross. Later his knees bent in contrition as he asked the Spirit for healing for his heart. Now the final blow has smitten his face into the dust.

In that moment of time he finds himself residing in eternity in the mind of God. Of clay, the potter has formed a friend. They shall not depart.

He has come to the lowest point to which Christian doctrine can lead a man. But in his most subject humility, silent before his God and at the lowest moment of his conscious life he finds himself to have been known and loved by God in eternity.

GOD IS GOD

When you say to men "God is God"
They seem to see the truth and nod.
And when you say "He can do anything"
They will surely like that orthodox ring.

But when you say "*HE* chose"
Their minds begin to close.
For they have learned by rote,
Mankind has the deciding vote.

It matters not what Scriptures say;
Modern man must have his sway.
"Let God be God but not over me!"
In every man Adam shouts his plea.

For in each man there speaks a voice,
"Thank you, please, I'll make my own choice.
Let God be God and do what I say.
If He won't, then I won't play."

14

Then he boasts and appeals to reason,
"I chose God and I'm not teasin'."
"Reason will answer," men declare,
"We chose Him, that makes Him fair."

Some never learn that they've got it wrong;
They just keep singing that tired old song.
Reason wins over every decree.
God does not decide they all agree.

"He has no rights over man's clay.
We saved ourselves on a lucky day."
This is the pride of Adam's whole race,
"We need just a little of thy divine grace."

And that pretty much tells man's story;
If he needs little grace, he gets much glory.
Except that Truth just keeps on repeating,
"Don't you know My grace you're depleting?"

So, my friend ——

When you learn your opinion to shun,
You'll probably find an "election" you've won.
You'll hear, far above reason's noise and din,
A voice, "My will too needed to be born again."

CHAPTER THREE
GOD MADE ALL THE LINKS

Some have relegated the issues of election and the Sovereignty of God to the category of the irrelevant. Their reasoning is that no one can really know much about this subject anyway, so why debate? Others feel that it bears only on the character of God who is infinite, therefore, the subject defies our finite minds. It is to be granted that God is infinite and no one can understand Him in all His dimensions. But the fact is that He has chosen to reveal much about Himself and His ways with man. And we are perfectly within our realm to study what He has revealed. In fact, there is a holy duty binding us to do so. The presence of a revelation about our God, to whom we owe all, obligates us to pursue our knowledge of Him by diligent study, to speak where it speaks, to be silent where it is silent. If eternal life is to "know and have fellowship with God" surely we must know who He is and what He is like if this fellowship is to be valid. Moreover, there are beneficial practical effects upon the believer to be gained by such a study. Paul told Timothy that "All scripture is inspired of God and is profitable...." Believing this to be true and that the right understanding of the Word of God does indeed cause Christian growth and "equip men for good works" we must know the truth. For if we leave out any of the truth as God has revealed it we will be just that short in character and just that much less powerful in service. If the doctrine of election is really taught in the Bible we must know it so that our inner man may feel the force of this truth, whatever that force may be. And likewise we need the encouragement it will bring to our efforts to win the lost for Christ.

One of the most practical effects of the doctrine of unconditional election is that of the faith and assurance it produces in the believer's life. When once the believer realizes that he has been in the divine mind from eternity there dawns upon his consciousness a settled assurance which surpasses any security he has known on earth or in his previous faith. And this is the point of what Paul is saying to the Roman church in Romans 8:28-30. He desires them to know that since they were "marked off" (predestinated) for salvation by God before the world began they will surely be glorified by God to bear the image of Christ. And since nothing can stand in the way of the will of the Sovereign God they will without question be glorified into that image in the eternity to come.

If a man can once see himself as being chosen on an unconditional basis before the world began, it will then be no problem to him to see himself glorified in the future with no possible event or trouble having the capacity to prevent it. Such a vision is Paul's goal in Romans 8:28-30. It remains for us to demonstrate this proposition.

Let us first read the text as it comes from the King James Version:

> And we know that all things work together for good to them that love God, to them who are the called according to his purpose.

> For whom he did foreknow he also did predestinate to be conformed to the image of his son, that he might be the firstborn among many brethren.

> Moreover, whom He did predestinate, them He also called; and whom He called, them He also justified; and whom He justified, them He also glorified. What shall we then say to these things? If God be for us, who can be against us?

These are majestic words. They connect the Christian to a God who chose him and despite tribulation, distress, and peril will not be prevented from having his ultimate will in that child's life. That may seem strong to some. But is that not Paul's intention? He sounds definite when he says, "All things work together for good to them that love God and are called according to his purpose." He speaks from the perspective of the divine plan, not from the standpoint of what man is doing for himself. Notice that he speaks of God's activity in foreknowledge, God's decision in predestination, God's calling, justification and glorification. It is God's activity and God's activity alone which is the subject of the message.

Paul is showing that there are five links in the chain of redemption: Foreknowledge, Predestination, Calling, Justification and Glorification. God foreknew those whom He wanted to be His. He marked them off (predestinated) to be His and to be conformed to the image of His Son, Jesus Christ. Then in the proper time He called them and made them willing to come to Christ. When they came He justified them by imputing to them righteousness. And as the final and culminating action of His grace upon them He glorified them (note the past tense, for it is already accomplished in the divine mind).

17

Furthermore, he is clearly stating that all the links are forged by God; they are not of human origin. It is not a weak chain. Not one link will fail. All of those who were predestinated were called, all who were called were justified, and all who were justified were glorified. The links do not grow smaller as dropouts reduce their size. All who were foreknown and marked off are present in the action of each link and are glorified in the end. This is precisely Paul's purpose; to show that without the loss of any, all who were chosen in the beginning were made into the image of the Son in glorification. His thought will not allow us to provide for the defeat of the divine purpose by the loss of any.

That this is the true thought of Paul is evident in the manner in which he writes. The repetition of the words "whom" and "them" prove this to be the fact. Look at verse 30. *"whom* he did predestinate, *them* he also called; and *whom* he called, *them* he also justified; and *whom* he justified; *them* he also glorified." The same persons are taken up by each repetition of the word *whom* and carried forward to the word *them* so that there is no fluctuation or loss in the prosecution of the divine purpose. All of the "foreknown" persons are included in the last link of glorification. In the end all of the chosen, without the loss of any, are glorified. God is not to be thwarted.

We must now look at the word *foreknowledge* in verse 29 to discover its real meaning. If it does indeed signify a choice made by God based upon his foreknowledge of what men would do, then unconditional election is not a scriptural doctrine. But if foreknowledge is something other than God's previewing of human response to the Gospel then unconditional election stands. Not one link in the chain of actual redemption is of our forging—or the whole indeed would be fragile.

The issue is really solved in Romans Nine where Paul declares that the choices of God are made prior to birth and without consideration of human character. Romans Nine is where Paul addresses the issue of the conditions of election. And he states the unconditionalness of election so emphatically that an election based upon man's choice or character cannot be allowed to be imputed anywhere it is not patent in the text. To impute it where it is not obvious is to write our thoughts upon the Divine Word. Nevertheless, this is often done with Romans 8:29. In spite of the fact that Paul says nothing about *what God foreknew,* men supply their own thoughts according to their own theological thought. As if the Word of God had left something out, men feel obligated to explain the divine action. And as if the foreknowledge of God must have had some humanly understandable rationale to it men supply "faith" or "man's choice" as that which God foreknew. It is worth reminding ourselves here that Paul says nothing about what God foreknew, except that he foreknew people. Paul says: "For whom he did foreknow, he also did predestinate."

So much attention has been focused upon the word *foreknowledge* that we must look into it for its best or most precise meaning in the text. But I would like to say that even without a discussion of the word foreknowledge, the issue is completely settled by Paul's declarations in Romans Nine. It cannot be that Paul would teach unconditional election in Romans Nine and conditional election in Romans Eight. And he doesn't. So we must be very careful when we are tempted to supply our own thoughts as to what foreknowledge means in Romans 8:29.

Certainly the word cannot mean God's omniscience by which he looked forward into time and saw who would respond to the Gospel. This is forbidden by the Word of God. For the Bible puts the "appointment" to salvation chronologically before faith (Acts 13:48):

> . . . and when the Gentiles heard this they were glad, and glorified the Word of the Lord: And as many as were ordained to eternal life believed.

There is no mistaking the meaning of Luke's words. He is stating categorically that faith in the Word of God comes after and is the effect of the choice of God. He can mean nothing else but this. To supply the thought of conditional election to Luke's historical record is ludicrous. It is ridiculous to allow his thought to be rendered: *"As many as God saw beforehand would believe did believe."* Luke did not interrupt his historical account of the critically important life of the early church to pat God on the back for his ability to see the future. But that is exactly what we have here if we interpret this verse according to conditional election. It is nothing more than saying, "Well, folks, many people were saved in Antioch of Pisidia, but it didn't surprise God, he knew it already. You sure can't put anything over on God." Luke most assuredly was not trying to give us a quick lesson on God's foresightedness. He was, rather, accounting for the results according to the theology of the day. He knows that the results cannot be accounted for by preaching alone, even though the preaching is truthful and anointed. He knows that faith cannot be credited to man's will. "It is not of him that willeth or of him that runneth, but of God who showeth mercy." How then did it happen that men believed? Because they were appointed to eternal life and when the Gospel was preached to them they were called out of death into life and they believed. Their faith was due to divine appointment. Their salvation can only be credited to the election of God. The missionary labors of Paul and his group were necessary. The preaching was essential. But when the preaching is over and the results are tallied, as best men can tally them, the ultimate explanation and accounting must reckon with the choice and appointment of God. Faith comes after and is the result of, not the cause of, election. Therefore, foreknowledge is not omniscience "looking into the future" as it makes up its mind what to do.

But what does foreknowledge mean? One concept of the word is that it means "foredecision." Handley G. C. Moule, in his commentary on Romans 8:29 translates it this way, "for whom He knew beforehand." He offers this explanation, "for whom He knew beforehand, with fore-knowledge which, in this argument, can mean nothing short of foredecision—no mere foreknowledge of what they would do, but rather of what He would do for them."

This definition of the word "foreknowledge" certainly appears to coincide with its use in Acts 2:23 and I Peter 1:2,20. Acts 2:23 reads, *"Him being delivered by the determinate counsel and foreknowledge of God, ye have taken, and by wicked hands have crucified and slain."* I Peter 1:2, 20 reads, *"elect according to the foreknowledge of God the Father..."* and *"who verily was foreordained (foreknowledge in the Greek) before the foundation of the world, but was manifest in these last times for you."*

The word "foreknowledge" occurs five times in the New Testament according to *Strong's Exhaustive Concordance of the Bible.* These references are: Acts 2:23, Romans 8:29, 11:2, I Peter 1:2, 20. The English translation of the Greek renders the word "foreknowledge" in Acts 2:23, Romans 8:29, and I Peter 1:2. It is found as "foreknew" in Romans 11:2 and as "foreordained" in I Peter 1:20. The Greek word is *proginosko* in Romans 8:29, 11:2 and I Peter 1:20. The Greek word is *prognosis* in Acts 2:23 and I Peter 1:2. Both Greek words are compound words made up of the Greek word for "prior to," or "in front of," *pro*; and Greek word for "to know," *ginosko. Ginosko* is capable of other connotations, among them are the following: allow, be aware of, feel, knowledge, perceive, and to understand. Strong offers the simple definition of *to know beforehand,* i.e., to foresee. He also suggests "forethought."

In his book, *Biblico-Theological Lexicon,* Cremer suggests a meaning drawn from the word itself. He says that "*ginosko* in New Testament Greek often denotes a personal relationship between the person and the object known—to suffer oneself to be determined thereby; for anything is known only so far as it is of importance to the person knowing and has an influence upon him so that a personal relationship is established between the knowing subject and the object known.

"The prefix *pro* to this word simply carried us back to an anterior period, and here it denotes that the *ginoskein* is already present in the divine decree before its manifestation in history; i.e., the union takes place between God and the objects of His sovereign grace. Hence we may render *whom God hath beforehand entered into fellowship with.* Thus the word is complete in itself and needing no addition from without. This view also preserves the distinction between foreknowledge and foreordination. The former, foreknowledge, being an act of conscious perception, the latter, foreordination, of specific volition."

The *International Standard Bible Encyclopedia* offers this commentary on Romans 8:29,30 under its discussion of the word "Foreknowledge:"

> In Romans 8:29,30 the word "foreknow" occurs in immediate connection with God's predestination of the objects of salvation. Those whom God foreknew, He also did predestinate to be conformed to the image of His Son. Now the foreknowledge in this case cannot mean a mere prescience or foresight of faith (Meyer, Godet) or love (Weiss) in the subjects of salvation, which faith or love is supposed to determine the Divine predestination. This would not only contradict Paul's view of the absolutely sovereign and gracious character of election, but it is diametrically opposed to the context of this passage. These verses form a part of the encouragement which Paul offers his readers for their troubles, including their own inward weakness. The apostle tells them that they may be sure that all things work together for good to them that love God; and these are defined as being those whom God has called in accordance with His purpose. Their love to God is evidently their love as Christians, and is the result of a calling which itself follows from an eternal purpose, so that their Christian love is simply the means by which they may know that they have been the subjects of this call. They have not come within the sphere of God's love by their own choice, but have been "called" into this relationship by God, and that in accordance with an eternal purpose on His part (p.1130).

Now, we may offer some conclusions regarding the meaning of foreknowledge which are based upon our study into the occurrence of the word in the Bible and the definitions and discussions offered by scholars. We may conclude firstly that the word foreknowledge never has as its object something seen in man which could be the basis of God's choice. And if it is not there in the text we must forbid ourselves to supply it even when reason cries for it. We must stop where God stops.

21

Secondly, we may suggest that the word is closely linked with the decision making processes of God. In referring to the death of Christ in I Peter 1:20, Peter uses the word foreknowledge to express the "foreordination" of this event. That foreknowledge means a plan and appointment in this passage is obvious. Peter would be guilty of saying nothing if he was merely referring to God's foresight of the Cross. He is magnifying grace and the cost of our redemption in these words. He declares that Calvary is not an act of desperation but one of design, even eternal design(Revelation 13:8). Calvary's love is magnified by the fact that God consciously determined to pay for our sin. Again Peter points to the meaning of foreknowledge as "foredecision" in Acts 2:23 where he says that Chirst was delivered up by *the determinate counsel and foreknowledge of God...."*

We must simply refuse to allow the concept of election in Romans 8 and 9 to be construed as God's foreknowledge of who would believe in Christ, thus making His choice of them dependent on their choice of Him. Moule says most accurately, "The doctrine of the Choice of God, in its sacred mystery, refuses—so we humbly think—to be explained away so as to mean in effect little but the choice of man." We must recognize that we make the doctrine teach the "choice of man" if we accept conditional election. And in the end we weaken the five links in the chain of redemption by making the very first of them dependent upon man and his will.

The very certainty which Paul desires to place within the mind of believers is that preservation amidst suffering and trials is not dependent upon man's choice or will or power. In other Scriptures there are many admonitions to stay firm in faith and to endure suffering. That is our responsibility. But in Romans 8 Paul is looking at the issue from the Divine side and is declaring that the issue is guaranteed to the true believer by the power of God. And that is why man's will must not be allowed to intrude. Paul does not consider it as affecting the divine activity and neither should we. Man is thought of only as the recipient of God's labor and grace. Paul declares the certainty of glorification because of its being rooted in the eternal purposes of the Omnipotent, Sovereign God. It is certain that the believer will be conformed to the image of Christ for that is what God originally determined to do and nothing can stand against Him. Considering that He is God, no other conclusion is possible. "What shall we then say to these things? If God be for us, who can be against us?"

Paul does not allow the human will to be a factor in any way. How weak verse 31 becomes, if man's choice is at the basis of God's choice. How puny to talk about the decrees of God and all the while to be thinking in the back

22

of one's mind that behind these decrees is the human will. The concept of God's sovereignty and power is weakened in its effect upon us if we accept the position of conditional election; for there is no exhilaration or encouragement in conditional election. How can I be encouraged if God's sovereignty over me is no stronger than my own human resolve? My confidence in God's power would then never rise above my estimate of my own will. This is exactly why the faith of many believers is weak. For their faith is nothing more than faith in faith. They believe that they are kept by their ability to hang on to Him, not by the fact that He is holding them. Their faith is measured by their will and resolve. When in reality faith does not measure itself by its possessor's ability to will or believe but by its object. Abraham's faith became strong because he knew His God and believed that He was able to perform what He had promised. Faith can never be any stronger than the object upon which it rests. If at the foundation of the divine purposes there is human will, then faith can never be any stronger or more dynamic than that human will. If the purposes of God are subject to the whims and weaknesses of the will of man, then that faith will always be mastered by the whims and weaknesses of man. Even though that man entertain great and noble ideas of his God, in the end his God will be subject to that man's own ability to will and resolve. And when man looks upon his election as being the result of his own choice then his glorification becomes no more secure than the power of his own resolve. And this is what the Bible will not allow. Paul has taken it out of man's hands by showing that not just glorification but faith itself is the result of the Sovereignty of God.

The whole purpose of Paul in Romans 8:28-30 is defeated by conditional election. For if man entered the first link of foreknowledge by his own choice then may he not drop out as he passes through any of the other links by his own choice? By his repetition of the words *whom* and *them,* Paul has answered this question. There are no dropouts. All of those involved in the foreknowledge and predestination are in the end glorified. The text will allow no other interpretation. But the man who feels his choice caused God's choice will never experience the thrill of this. For having entered on his own, he feels he may depart on his own when some alien force overwhelms his will or his will gives out.

Allowing election to be taught and understood as conditional removes all the assurance, thrill, and glory from the word. And this occurs whether we are fully conscious of it or not. For this reason the great biblical words of election and predestination are virtually never used by many Christians. They are meaningless and valueless because they mean nothing more than

23

"Man choosing God so that God would choose man." The writer has lived his entire Christian life in churches where the truth of election is not believed and to this day has only heard one full sermon on the subject of election. Furthermore, the words, election and predestination, though divinely inspired, never appear in books, literature, or sermons where election is not taught to be unconditional. Nor have the passages in Romans 8 and 9 dealing with election ever been properly preached if preached at all. Why? Because it is meaningless and futile to speak of an election which is based upon the will of man. There is no glory there. For the attention is taken from God's love which would choose a man and make a believer out of him to the man who decided on his own to become a believer. There is no love and mercy. For instead of the magnanimity of God's love reaching out to those who are living in hostility against Him, we have men seeking and choosing Him on their own. There is nothing divine or glorious here. For men do their daily business on the same basis and we are accustomed to it. Man bases his commercial and personal transactions upon the merit and worth of others. If God does the same, then why shout about it. There is nothing divinely loving, or romantically exciting, or overwhelmingly beautiful in such an idea as "I first loved Him, then He loved me." And hence no one talks about it except once in a while to try to harmonize the Sovereignty of God and freedom of man, or to throw some new philosophical approach at it. That is why it is never talked about or preached. But just for a moment believe it as it really is, *"God's choice of you when you didn't even know him. God's love of you when you were in revolt against Him. God's making you alive when you were dead in sin, incapable of hearing his voice."* What romance, what beauty, what grace. What loveliness and mercy is discovered in the God who though being rebelled against, woos and wins the enemy.

And then what assurance to see that by His grace and His grace alone you were placed into the chain of redemption. Sovereign grace having put you there, it will be with you to the end.

I WAS LOVED BEFORE TIME

Before mother and father knew I might be on the way,

Before she ever held me close,

Before he ever taught me to work,

Before I had a name,

I was known and loved.

Before I was ever a probability to them I was a reality to God.

I WAS LOVED BEFORE TIME

Before I met my first slobbering friend crawling toward my crib,

Before I ever rode two on a bike,

Before I ever held a girl's hand,

Before the first buddy,

Before the first "best friend,"

There was One Friend who knew me well.

I WAS LOVED BEFORE TIME

Long before I began this adult life,

Before I knew that life was hard,

When every week had its pain

And its dollar quota,

Before I knew that life would be

Swinging a hammer,

Sitting behind a desk,

Before I knew that life was demanding,

There was One who planned it that way because He loved me.

I WAS LOVED BEFORE TIME

Before my conscience ever hurt,

Before my sins glared back at me,

Before my lostness became apparent,

Before I ever began to move back to Him,

HE KNEW ME. HE LOVED ME.

HE CHOSE ME BEFORE TIME BEGAN.

THAT SPEAKS RATHER WELL FOR MY FUTURE!!

CHAPTER FOUR

MAN'S WILL CANNOT ACCOUNT FOR SALVATION

We have considered two important passages from the writings of Paul, Romans 8:28-30 and Romans 9. The truth of unconditional election has been proved from Romans 9. Its place in giving us an overwhelming assurance of our ultimate salvation is described for us in Romans 8. There we have found that we were in the mind of God in eternity and that our present and final redemption reaches back to that point. It is certain in that it rests in the power of a Sovereign God to accomplish what He alone has determined to do. We can rejoice with joy unspeakable as we see ourselves as a part of His plan. But a question comes to our minds which must be answered: "*How did God work upon my heart and will to cause me to want to enter the stream of His purposes? How do I account for my own conversion? If it was not my will choosing God, then what was it?*" To see the scriptural answers to these questions let us look at the Prologue of the Gospel of John (John 1:1-18).

The critical verses for our consideration are verses 9-13; but it will help us to set the scene if we consider the place and purpose of the prologue. The prologue, we must remember, is an introduction to the book. It is written, along with the rest of John's Gospel, many years after the events described took place. Merril Tenney tells us that the Gospel of John was probably written toward the close of the first century which would place its date some forty to sixty years after the events it records. John, then, writes from notes and memories the historical account of Jesus, the Son of God. His aim is to provide evidence that Jesus was indeed the Son of God and his desire is that when men see these "signs" they will believe and "have life through his name." The narrative of John's gospel begins with verse 19 of chapter one and continues through verses 24, 25 of chapter 21, where John signs off. From chapter 1:19—21:23 we have historical happenings as John viewed them. These things occurred before his eyes. Many years after they happened he sat down to record them. But his mind is full of more than narrative. His mind is thinking of all the times he has told the story of

27

Christ. How often down through the decades he has repeated just the things he is going to write about. "What an amazing story it is," he muses. He finds that he cannot just begin with the narration. He must make some preliminary remarks.

His thoughts first turn to the true nature of this One "which was from the beginning, which we have heard, which we have seen with our eyes, which we have looked upon, and our hands have handled, of the Word of life...." He was then and is now convinced that this One was the Son of God. His narrative must wait. First he must express his belief. *In the beginning was the word and the word was with God and the word was God.*" This expression was not something John had ever heard Jesus say in so many words; it was his own personal conclusion about the One with whom he had lived for three years. The Spirit of God made him write it down. The evidence of the narrative will follow but first John must express the only possible meaning of the historical account, *Jesus is the Christ, the Son of God.* John explains that Jesus had always been for He was eternal. He was the Creator. He was life and whenever He was living with men He became a light to their souls. He shined His light into the darkness but the darkness did not only not comprehend it but resisted it.

John continues his introduction by telling us that God had prepared a special man to introduce this Light to the world. His name also was John, the Baptist, and while he was not the Light himself, he was one of the first to recognize it and point it out to men.

All of this is recalled clearly as John with the Holy Spirit begins to write the story. But something else is upon John's mind as he writes this introduction. He cannot help but think of how many times he has told the story he will now write. To bands of Christians. To doubting souls. To pagans deep in superstition and idolatry. He has rehearsed it before crowds gathered in synagogues and homes. The church in Ephesus has heard him tell the beloved story so many times they almost feel they were there when it happened. He recalls those occasions down through the years and remembers that there were always two different reactions to the message. The Holy Spirit prompts him to write about these two responses and we find them in John 1:9-13. The first response of men was always tragic. Though Jesus was the Light which lightens every man who comes into the world, though He was in the very world He had created, men did not acknowledge Him. Not the world at large, nor even His very own, the Jews. He could tell the story again and again in different times and manners but there was this part of humanity which would not understand or be receptive. That always brought sorrow to John. But the sorrow was countered by the response of the other group. For as John recounts the years and the ministries of preaching, he sees the countless number who heard and received the truth. The message caught hold. It seemed to fit them like a seed in good soil. John could always predict the results of such acceptance: "those who received the truth would begin to live and act like sons of God." There was a new authority in their life. The right of sonship had become theirs. They no longer were just "creatures" of God; they were "children of God." This always happened when men and women believed on His Name.

But why did these believe? What accounts for the fact of their openness and receptivity to the truth? Why was their soil ready for the seed? Were they better? Did they think through the issues and decide that they must choose him? Did they have some propensity toward God? Did their heredity or basic personality predispose them to faith? Were these better or wiser people then the rejectors?

John's answer to these questions is found in verse thirteen: *"Which were born, not of blood, nor of the will of the flesh, nor of the will of man, but of God."* He says that there is only one valid way to account for the faith of these who were saved by the message, *their faith and salvation was the result of being born of God.* It cannot be attributed to "blood," or human descent and heredity. There is nothing in the genes and chromosomes of human life which makes man choose God. Grace does not run in the blood of some. Nor can faith be accounted for by the will of the flesh. John agrees with Paul here, "The carnal mind is enmity with God." The flesh which is hostile and rebellious toward its Maker will surely not receive His Son. The natural man may seek many things but he will never seek God (Romans 3:11). None of the historical accounts of nations or biographies of men ever give a trace of one man who has sought out God due to the desire of the flesh. But John takes us even deeper than this into the list of impossible causes. It is his exact and Spirit-corroborated testimony that human salvation cannot be accounted for by the *will of man.* The will of man will never choose what that man himself hates. The will of a man is the servant of his heart and his ambitions. The will chooses what the man himself loves. The will declines what that man hates. The will may be free to choose but it will not opt for any choice which does not agree with the stomach it feeds. A man may walk into an ice cream store and look at the long list of available flavors. "Vanilla, Chocolate, Coconut-pineapple, Orange sherbet, Peppermint, Strawberry." His will can be exercised whichever way he desires. The same quarter will buy any flavor he chooses. But when the choice is made and the money laid down he will choose the flavor he likes. His will will serve his appetite. And so the will of man serves the appetite of man who chooses against God because he disdains God. It has always been so because that is the nature of man. The fact that some come to the Light and are made into the Sons of God cannot be accounted for by the will of man.

How do we then account for the fact that some do believe? *They are born of God.* God has put it into their hearts to come(John 6:65). Their faith is the result of God's work upon their souls. Their hunger for God is the result of the 'quickening' of the Spirit of God. Paul agrees with this, "When we were dead in sins, hath quickened us together with Christ" (Ephesians 2:5).

The will of man can account for rejection and refusal of free eternal life through Jesus Christ but cannot account for acceptance of Christ. This is John's witness concerning those who do receive and are made into new creatures! *They were born of God.*

Some will be deeply upset and troubled at this thought. But have we not noticed the same response to our witnessing and preaching as John did? There are those times when the clearest and most anointed preaching of the Gospel leaves men unmoved. Sometimes we blame ourselves for this. We wonder what is wrong. Let us remember that every apostle and preacher of the Christian ages has felt the same bitter taste: to tell a man of the free gift of eternal life, the love-price the Saviour paid, and have him stand there as if it didn't matter; to labor in a missionary field where culture and language are against the preacher and feel the power of darkness which cannot see even a trace of the Light. Remember, John felt that too.

But John felt something else that we experience. From behind the pulpit the story is being told once again, from behind the pew there is an interest upon that face that speaks of Life. Neither "raised hand" nor "altar call" is needed, for new creaturehood has reached into a lost soul during the telling. Sitting in the pew they have "entered the second time into the womb and been born again." No man saw it happen. The wind just blew where it wanted to and heaven had a new citizen, not unknown by God. One more name on heaven's roster was circled. Praise the Lord. "Was it my sermon?" I ask. That was indeed part of it. But the best sermon is called by the Bible "watering" and "planting." It is God who gives the increase. Only God can touch the soul.

"If it is all this certain and sovereign, then why don't we just quit preaching?" some would say. But that is to forget the place of preaching. Preaching is not just man's effort to persuade the human will. It is a means ordained by God to create within the dead soul life, within the blind soul sight, within the sick soul health. Preaching is divine creation. We marvel that God can use men like He does to speak creative words to dead souls,

30

but He does. When the elect preacher preaches the truth to the elect soul, the chemistry of Divine sovereignty and gospel preaching produces life from death. The preacher has but to do his duty and be faithful to the truth, being careful not to take the credit for what he has not done, bringing the dead to life. Knowing his place he can have greater confidence and greater faith and joy than ever before for the results are in higher hands. Resurrection power is in his message by the edict of God. Many will reject, but some will receive, and that faith is both the joy of the preacher and the glory of God who raises the dead. Far from being a discouragement the doctrine of election should be an encouragement to the preacher of the Gospel. Let him think of it for a few minutes and he will see that he cannot fail to win the lost if he just preaches the truth. God has chosen him to go and bring forth fruit.

His responsibility is to declare the truth. And this he must do. For it is the truth which is light. And it is the light which draws the elect. John 3 speaks of this phenomenon. In verse 20 John tells us that those who practice evil do not come to the light because it would expose their evil actions and hearts. In verse 21 he explains why some do come to the light. They come because they are already practicing truth. And since they love the truth they want more of it. Even their actions show that they are truth-seekers. And so they come to the light that it may be shown that their deeds are produced by God. While the light condemns those who do not seek it, it draws those who are already "doing truth" because God is working in them. This explains why some of the greatest conversions are unexciting and undramatic. They have been "doing truth" for years as God worked upon their hearts. Their hearing and acceptance of the ultimate truth of Christ is a step for which they have been prepared by the grace of God. It marks no traumatic movement in their soul for they have been always moving in that direction. More than one saint of God has confessed that their hunger and love for God has preceded their conversion by years. So much so, that they cannot remember the time when they did not feel a desire for God. This is what John is saying to us. There are those in our communities prepared by God. They are fish ready to bite. God is working upon their minds even now to prejudice them toward the words that you will preach. You have but to preach the truth to them and they will recognize the light and come to it.

It is indeed a "prevenient grace." But not one which unscripturally magnifies man's will. Not one which sees the grace of God working upon a man to enable him to believe if he wants to and then making its choice of that man only a reaction to the man's choice. But rather, a foregoing grace which gives a man such a love for the truth and God that that man's own sinful nature and hostility toward God are overcome and he will be saved when he hears the Gospel. That such elect people are in the world is the testimony of Scripture. That they will come to Christ and be saved is the guarantee of the words of Christ: *"all that the father giveth me shall come to me, and him that cometh to me I will in no wise cast out."* We may feel the confidence of this truth and its help to our preaching if we will look to the sovereign will of God and not to the will of man. Have confidence in the preaching of the truth. Have faith in the God who raises the dead. Preach and live the light; men will come to it.

FREE-WILL IS A PILL
I JUST CAN'T SWALLOW.

KNOWING ME AS I DO
IT SOUNDS SORT OF HOLLOW.

I KNOW I AM FREE
TO CHOOSE WHAT I WOULD.

BUT I NEVER SEEM
TO CHOOSE WHAT I SHOULD.

CHAPTER FIVE

PREACHING COURAGE AND CREDENTIALS

We have spoken of the loss of power in the concept of election when it becomes nothing more than man's choice of God—how that concept robs the believer of faith in God and causes him to place faith in his own faith and will. The sovereignty of God then becomes a weak thing. Even God becomes weak to that man. (Again, we speak as men.) God must be something less than true God if all of his plans and efforts are subject to the veto of man. And this is precisely what the doctrine of conditional election makes God out to be, a member of the executive branch who must submit his proposals to the legislative branch, which is man. After man debates, modifies and conditions the proposals, they are then carried out by a submissive God. It is small wonder then, that we know so little about the really Great God of the Bible, the Great "I Am" who *"works all things according to the counsel of his own will"* and answers to no one. We are so busy trying to make God tolerable and attractive to men we have emasculated Him. Not willing to face Him as the Bible reveals Him, we make excuses for His behavior as if God needed defense. And then having made our excuse, we find that we are bound by it. For having made it we believe it and find ourselves with a lesser God than we might have. One who must first submit to man before He moves. One who must first clear His sovereignty with a human congress. It should be no surprise then that Christians are shaky. Some cling to materialism to their hurt. Others must have every word of prophetic Scripture spoon fed to them so that they will have no doubts about what exactly will happen in the future. They can't leave some of the incidentals to God for after all He may not be able to handle it alone. Many live from one emotional experience to another. These are some of the ruinous effects of conditioning God's sovereignty to man's will.

There is yet, however, an even more disastrous effect. That is the influence of the thought of a limited God upon the mind and courage of the preacher. Having no sovereign God he feels alone in his labors. He must find the lost on his own. He must have promotions to draw them. He must produce "high class musicals" to attract the unwilling to hear about their God. He must lean heavily upon gimmicks to help the dead soul come to life and believe. Furthermore, he must be delicate in his preaching. He would not want to offend someone who was just about convinced. That man who was just about ready to "give his life to Christ" might be upset and turned off when the truth is really preached. Sermons must be aesthetic, intellectual, psychologically oriented, and above all short. For that is what the natural man will find enticing. "Be careful about the anointing of God upon your soul. Don't get carried away with the glory of it all. You might say something before you have a chance to monitor it. And above all, don't preach over twenty minutes." Such are the doubts and misgivings of the preacher who has not found his God. The work is his and his alone. *He* must find the lost. *He* must move their will. *He* must bring them to Christ. And *He* must keep them in Christ. He must, therefore, keep them blessed and happy. He must adjust his message to their ability to hear and believe. For he cannot count on the supernatural quickening of the dead, and the renewing and livening of the saint. Having made God dependent upon man, his message now becomes man-centered.

Jesus prevented all of this with his disciples when He told them in John 15:16:

> *"Ye have not chosen me, but I have chosen you, and ordained you, that ye should go and bring forth fruit, and that your fruit should remain: that whatsoever ye shall ask of the father in my name, He may give it to you.*

These words were spoken to the disciples as a part of the last instructions Jesus would give them about their future ministries. It must be rooted in their minds, He knew, that they did not place themselves into the Christian life or into the Christian ministry. To put the initiative into their hands would leave the working out of their ministries in their hands. That would be disastrous. Jesus must make them aware that the arduous and impossible life they were about to begin was something for which they had been chosen and specially ordained. Only then would they be adequate for it. When the days of persecution and suffering came how fatal it would be for them to begin to look upon their own motives and ambitions as the source of the calling. The vacillation and misgivings which would follow them would make them impotent if their preachings were the result of their own abilities or choices. How could they face a pagan world? How could they face even the people of Jerusalem who would kill them as they had

34

their Lord? How could they preach the Gospel to the same people who had crucified the Lord of Glory if there were not a sovereign God who would raise the dead to faith? They must never think of their calling as self-initiated. Nor would God have any true minister of the Gospel think of himself as self-employed. There will be no conviction of divine mission in the man who knows not the sovereignty of God. There will be no authority in the words of the man who appointed himself. He will never impress anyone as a "spokesman of God."

It was conclusive in the mind of Paul that he was chosen and commissioned by God (Gal. 1:1): *"Paul, an apostle, (not of men, neither by man, but by Jesus Christ, and God the Father, who raised him from the dead)."* Nor did he feel such calling and commissioning took place on the Damascus Road (Gal. 1:15): *"But when it pleased God, who separated me from my mother's womb, and called me by his grace, to reveal his son in me...."* In his mind he saw himself as an apostle from the moment of his birth. It was a strange apprenticeship. But the centuries which have passed since then prove that God knows how to make a journeyman. No self-styled evangelist could have done what Paul did. To do an immortal work you must feel you have roots in eternity. No man who is unconscious of a divine supernatural call can do a great work for God. No man who is unconscious of an irresistible sovereignty moving through his life can work miracles of saving grace. Without the Sovereignty of God a man is left in his ministry armed with only his own wits. And wits don't raise many of the dead.

Jesus will not leave the disciples to their wits. He lets them know that the initiative was His. He chose them. He ordained them. It was His executive order that the dead should respond to the Gospel and come forth from their grave clothes.

How we need this conviction today! What boldness it begets! Peter can stand on the day of Pentecost and indict his hearers with having crucified Christ. He makes no effort to be conciliatory, except for the reconciling love which is in his heart. And when he is finished three thousand indicted souls are forever acquitted. Where does he get this boldness? He knows he is chosen. He cannot but speak the truth. The truth will draw these who are coming to the light. He sees no possible defeat of the sovereign purposes of God.

We need this conviction today for it produces the only possible encouragement in the hard places of Gospel work. A man once said to me, "If the doctrine of election is true, and the elect will surely come to Christ, I wish my parents would never have gone to that hard missionary field where they are ministering." His feeling was that they had given up much to be missionaries and it would not have been necessary if election were true. They could have done something less arduous. But that is to miss the point. The real application of election to our ministries is that wherever God may send us it is for the purpose of bearing fruit. And if the field is hard the guarantee is needed all the more lest despair set in. In the future these missionaries will be rewarded for their difficult labors. But now they may be convinced that their efforts and sacrifice cannot possibly be in vain for they are *ordained to bear fruit which remains.* .They did not put themselves on that field; God did, and not to frustrate them. If they can and will trace the initiative back to God, they will find a flood of hope in their field. No darkness or hardship will prevent their bearing fruit. And if their work does not show progress and health which would be typical of divine blessing, they can apply the pledge of sovereignty to their prayers. They can fill their prayers with argument,

> *Father in Heaven, you chose me for this church; you ordained that I bear fruit here. Now I don't think either you or I can be happy with the little bit of fruit that is growing here. You have said that you would be glorified when I bear much fruit. Now, Father, help me. It is your work. You put the plan together. You put me on this field to be fruitful your word tells me. And I am asking now to be made fruitful. Jesus said you would do what I ask in His name. Now, Father, it is time for us to reproduce. Amen.*

Dear Brothers and Sisters, the same God who put you in your field will hear your cry. And if you continue to rub that argument into the ears of God you will bring forth much fruit. The sovereign God will be working into the chosen vessel the capacity for bearing more fruit.

It is essential in time of hardship and worldly indifference to have an awareness of a call of God which roots itself in the eternal and irresistible counsels of God. The ministry of Jeremiah is a vivid illustration. For his times parallel ours. They were days when men were focusing upon the externals of religion. Their boast was in the presence of the Temple. They were materialistic and unconscious of the coming judgment. They did not heed the "book" found in Josiah's time; yet they superstitiously believed that it was protection (Jer. 8:8). In the midst of this disease and misery, God called Jeremiah. Jeremiah will preach for more than forty years with very little evidence of fruit. The prophet will weep and groan while he preaches, but the people will not hear him. How can you prepare a man for such a ministry? What do you say to a man whose calling will never cease to press tears from his eyes, who must look on while a nation commits suicide? Only one thing will sustain a preacher in such times and that is a consciousness of destiny. And so while Jeremiah is being called as a young man, God speaks to him: *"Before I formed thee in the belly I knew thee; and before thou camest forth out of the womb I sanctified thee, and I ordained thee a prophet unto the nations."* Jeremiah must see the origin of his commission as being in the eternal plan of the Almighty. He must not think it was teenage "promise" which made him God's choice. He must not feel it was an "aptitude" for the office of prophet which got him the job. He faced a lifetime of rejection and plots against his life. He must stand before kings and indict them. He must warn a nation of a coming disaster which they refuse to acknowledge. His message will be contradicted by the other prophets. There is no youthful "promise" which qualifies a man for such tasks. There is no "aptitude" for living out a calling which will cause a prophet to curse the day he was born. There is no human preparation to ready a man to be scorned by friends and apparently "mocked" by his God (Jer. 20). No, Jeremiah must see himself as destined to fill this onerous place. And he must be able to derive meaning and gratification from the fact that in doing so he is pleasing his God if no one else. Satisfaction will not come from results, there will be little of that. He will never be able to recline at the end of a decade and look out the window at the great chuch he has built. His converts will be few. There will be no soul-rewarding gratification to be found in revival of the masses. He will have to content himself with the joy of pleasing his God even if no one responds. He must know that he is doing that for which he was made.

The destiny for which God alone has fitted him will suffice him. He may protest his call by pointing to his youth and lack of eloquence (Jer. 1:6). But that won't dissuade the Caller. For it was not human ability or courage Jeremiah needed. He needed only trust in the divine words and presence. Not to be afraid but to speak what he heard was the confidence he gained from his call. He was not to be afraid to speak the message of God and even if it pleased no one but God, his task could be considered well done. Jeremiah carried out his call. Under such auspices any man could. And that is precisely the point of this message. God needs spokesmen. Men who will speak out with the force of the old prophets. Men who are conscious of a call to preach as the "oracles of God." Men who are bold. Men who follow Spurgeon's advice to "be afraid to be afraid." Men who feel that destiny has fitted them for their task, and who would rather sink into the mire (Jeremiah 38) than adapt their message to the whims of their hearers. They

37

have but one purpose and that is to please the one who called them before they were formed, to satisfy the prophetic urge which was conceived within their unborn substance. Such courage comes from credentials issued by the Sovereign God.

WHY DON'T YOU TOAST YOUR POST?

It's always been the same when Heaven calls a man;
The protests and argumehts seem almost identical.
In vain the preacher says, "I don't think I can."
It's almost a pattern in things prophetical.

The bush burned bright as Moses' shoes came off;
"Go to Pharaoh and free my people," The Lord said.
Now we almost laugh as we hear Moses scoff,
"Who? Me? My speech is bad, send someone in my stead."

But it was not in Moses' talent the challenge lay,
For God was not unaware of what He asked.
"Here's a rod, and a brother, that's my way.
Follow me, I will fit you for the task."

When Jeremiah first heard the voice of God
He argued so boldly it gives me a scare.
"I am too young such a dark path to trod.
I speak poorly and my nature is too fair."

But his youth and speech were to God no surprise.
God knew long before birth his tongue didn't work.
He might have even planned it, I surmise.
"Jeremiah, have courage, pay no mind to their smirk."

"Speak what I tell you, loud and clear.
You were chosen for this place long before birth.
Never let your heart be possessed by fear.
Give them my words and I will shake the earth."

This message is needed when we feel accidental
As we think over the call to our post.
This is the time to consider powers providential
And to remember we didn't pop up like toast.

38

CHAPTER SIX
DOES IT REALLY MATTER? HOW DOES IT MATTER?

There is a reaction to the preaching of the doctrine of unconditional election which is phrased with a shrug and a "ho-hum." "Does it really matter? Does the issue have any real significance to the task before us as Christians? Why don't we just go out and win souls? Why don't we just keep the message simple? Why raise such difficult questions? Why stir up an issue which is unimportant and inconsequential?" *But is it?* Can anything clearly revealed in the Word of God be inconsequential? Are we not commanded to "live by every word which *proceeds* out of the mouth of God?" And if we do not, will we not miss some of the vital nutrients for our spiritual life and warfare? Certainly we will. And it is obvious we are missing something when one looks at the shallowness of much Christian living and preaching. It almost appears that Christian living and preaching becomes irrelevant when sound Christian doctrine becomes irrelevant. The most practical book of the Bible, Proverbs, speaks wisdom to us when it says, *"Where there is no vision the people perish."* And it is true today; where there is no ministry of all the truth, where there is no "seer," people languish and perish. Much of the lethargy of believers today is due to the fact that they are not fully acquainted with the Sovereign God who chose them and called them to faith and sonship. Maintaining their own sovereignty they are lost by an awareness of their inability to do their part. Weary from trying to "help out God," men give up their dreams of conquering worlds for Christ.

It does matter and it matters greatly that this issue be faced by every believer. If only for the sake of being honest with the Word of God the issue must be understood. We must be honest with the Word of our God if we are to do well the work of our God. It is our only weapon to penetrate the hearts of men. To humble the proud. To regenerate the dead. To give light to those who stumble on and on in darkness. We cannot pierce the hard heart of man with a dull sword. Nor can the dim light of half-truths provide sufficient light in a world fogged with darkness. We must have all the truth to set men free.

In addition to gaining power to free these souls of men, there are other essential benefits to be gained from a proper understanding of the sovereign election of God. Two of these benefits are of great significance. The first of these two is the effect of the doctrine upon the individual and his knowledge of himself and how this affects his life with God. The second is the manner in which unconditional election influences our preaching, both in our concept of what it is and in the content of what we do indeed preach.

We will look first at the impact of the sovereignty of God upon the individual and consider what happens to man as his mind grapples with this immense thought. The initial effect of the sovereignty of God upon a believer is submission. Not a submission based upon his new knowledge that God is sovereign. But a submission produced by the experience of "allowing" God to be sovereign. This submission is produced by the process by which a man comes to understand the doctrine of election. He finds himself in a conflict which he must lose to win. The conflict is one that develops between his own thoughts as a man and the thoughts of God which come from the Word of God.

He finds that there is a great distance and difference between his own concepts and God's concepts. The issue was drawn up by Isaiah when he spoke of God's thoughts and man's thoughts: "For my thoughts are not your thoughts, neither are your ways my ways. For as the heavens are higher than the earth, so are my ways higher than your ways, and my thoughts than your thoughts." Here is where the battle lines are drawn. It is mind against mind. Man's thoughts against God's thoughts. Man's belief in his own sovereignty wrestling against the revealed fact of God's absolute Lordship. But it is more than just man's belief in his sovereignty which intensifies the struggle; it is his desire for sovereignty. In his struggle with election, man has returned to the garden and faces again the question, *"Whom shall I serve? Myself or God? Who shall have the ultimate voice? Who shall be allowed to speak and govern? My ideas or God's?"* And the battle rages. The lower ways and thoughts of man struggling to leave their imprint upon the higher ways of God. The natural mind of man fights fiercely. If he can only hold that election is conditional then God will be subject to him to some degree. The carnal man feels more comfortable when God is thought to be a partner rather than a sovereign.

And so we discover that the warfare is not just mental, it is spiritual. It is not just a matter of convincing the mind that the doctrine is taught in Scripture. That would be not too difficult. Such passages as Romans 9, Romans 8 and John 1:12,13; 6:44,65 demonstrate unconditional election to be true beyond doubt. Why then is it so difficult to apprehend the truth of

40

the Word? Because it is more than a mental struggle. The mind and heart of man do not want to give up their thoughts. The human heart is comfortable when it feels sovereign and the thought of such sovereignty is cherished. The lower thoughts of man protest the higher thoughts of God. The spirit of man is agitated by the opposition it feels from the Word of God. The battle is not alone in the intellect. The solution will not come alone from Bible study. While that is the source of the truth knocking at the door, only proper creaturely submission will open the door. Those who have fought through this issue will attest to the validity of these observations. Exegesis of the Word of God presented the truth to them but the spiritual resistance of the carnal mind refused to allow it in the door. The hostile mind clings to its lower thoughts. And therefore for man to come to an understanding of personal unconditional election he must not only open his mind to the Revealer of Truth but he must bend his knee to the Sovereign. In bending his knee he arrives at the proper posture for all creatures. He finds that the Spirit leads us into truth by helping us to lose battles.

The believer must be careful at this point. He may start to enjoy losing. Once having savored the clean, crisp air of God's "higher thoughts" he may never again hold out for his own low ground. He may be permanently persuaded that "God's ways are better than man's." Having at first shakily given a little ground to God, he may now turn it all over to Him and by losing the battles win the war.

In allowing his own thoughts to be overruled by God's thoughts he learns not only sovereignty but submission. He has learned that God's Word is a much better interpreter of God than is his own mind. From now on he will allow for the Divine veto upon his own ideas.

The knowledge of the doctrine of unconditional election influences the life of the believer in another very important way. It provides him with an understanding of his nature as man which he will never find in conditional election. As long as he persists in believing that "he first chose God" he will never find out who he really is. He will never probe the depths of his being. Only the man who sees himself as saved by the choice of God can say "By the grace of God I am what I am," with full meaning. And only that man will appreciate to the full the grace of God.

The man who sees himself as making the critical move toward God which made God respond to him will always have to give some credit for his redemption to his own will. This is true even if the idea of prevenient grace is taught. For prevenient grace means only that God brings men to a place where they can believe and accept Christ if they choose to. It describes a work in the lost man which gives him the capacity to believe. But the actual faith and receiving is something which the man does by an exercise of his own will. Therefore, his own will will always obtrude into the essential cause of his salvation. His ultimate accounting of his personal salvation will be, "When God drew me, I chose to respond." And therefore, he has both the grace of God and his own decision to thank.

Such is not the case with the man who knows his salvation came not by his own will but by the will of God. He recognizes that his human nature and will were leading him in hostility down a Damascus Road when grace intervened. He readily admits that "No man can come unto me, except it were given him of my Father." Charles Spurgeon had the perspective of the man who knows his own heart aright. He said,

> I must confess that I never would have been saved if I could have helped it. As long as ever I could, I rebelled, and revolted, and struggled against God. When He would have me pray, I would not pray, and when He would have me listen to the sound of the ministry, I would not. And when I heard and the tear rolled down my cheek, I wiped it away and defied Him to melt my soul. But long before I began with Christ, He began with me.

Mr. Spurgeon was forced to this conclusion about his own nature by learning the doctrine of election. Having acknowledged the biblical truth of unconditional election man is forced to definite conclusions about his own nature. No man can adopt the truth of election and at the same time hold to his own sovereignty or his ability to choose God. He cannot continue to think himself capable of seeking or choosing God when he understands that God chose him apart from his own will, deeds, or faith. Knowing this he has to abdicate his pretended throne. He must move elsewhere. When the believer sees God occupying the seat of the Sovereign Elector, he will then move to the chair of humility. He will see himself as he is. He will recognize that if the only way to be saved is for "God to put it into man's heart to come" then indeed his own heart must have been dead, void of spiritual desire, with no Godward movement (Rom. 3:11). And the only adequate accounting for his birth into the new life is that he was *born of God;* not of the will of the flesh nor man.

Only when the doctrine of election without human conditions is preached will the Christian come to this desirable biblical view of himself. Only then will he bow in humble adoration and confess *"How great thou art."* Only then will he move from the seat of sovereignty to the seat of humility. Only then will he bow into the dust and stay there for the remaining days of his journey. And only then will he bring forth the praise and fruit which comes solely from such humility.

42

This is not a humility put on or forced from man's lips. It is not a facade. It is not a role. Having seen himself as he is, man awakes every morning in the dust and finds his only glory is in his Lord. He has a built-in buffer against pride, which is his knowledge of his own heart. He cannot be fooled. He knows that all of these Godward movements of his soul were placed there by God. He cannot thank himself. In all honesty, without pretense or dramatic speech, he knows that he is what he is by the grace of God.

Humility will be encouraged but never found until one faces his sovereign Father and realizes that he was *born of God* and not by his own will. Humility may be taught but never experienced until the soul of the redeemed man knows that he was dead when he was called and blind when he began to see. No man wants to see himself in this light. But it is the biblical truth about man. And only the doctrine of unconditional election will force it upon our proud minds.

There is a further effect of the truth of election which relates to our preaching. Having come to a personal understanding of what he is in his own heart, the preacher is now ready to diagnose properly the real sickness of his hearers. Why should they be any different from him? Are not their hearts the same? If he was dead so are they. If he was hostile toward God so are they. If God had to "put it into his heart to come" then God will have to "put it into their hearts to come." If it took a miracle of divine grace to give him new life then he will not expect that they will come alive through a nice little devotional talk on Sunday morning. He will recognize that they need more than an inspirational song and an emotional anecdote; they need resurrection. Resuscitation will not do it for they are dead. The power of the living God must be generated into their hearts. The preacher will not spend his time talking about the free will of sinners. He knows the will of a dead man can never choose life.

When Jesus came to Lazarus He did not recommend that Lazarus exercise his free will to make himself alive. He did not say to Lazarus, "Now, Lazarus, you know you're in pretty bad shape, don't you? I'm going to do something for you. But I need your help. First of all, I want you to know that you have a free will. And you are going to have to exercise your free choice when I give the invitation. Now if you don't do this I really can't help you. The only way you can come alive again is if you help me get you out of this grave. Now you just nod your head if you understand. That's not a very good nod. In fact, I'm not sure you even moved. But I'll assume you are listening because at least you are not fidgeting."

It's ridiculous to think of Jesus doing that. He knew Lazarus was dead.

His soul had been in Hades for four days. For four days no living current had operated his brain. His heart had not pumped. His blood had broken down and he smelled bad. He was dead and all those downwind knew it. But then came the regal command, *"Lazarus, come forth."* The voice was heard beyond Bethany in the mysterious abode of Sheol. A four-day visitor was asked to be excused from Abraham's bosom. But what about the body? Living spirits cannot inhabit smelly carcasses. An electric shock awakened the brain. The heart muscle convulsed. Blood moved through suddenly soft arteries. Red and white cells marched to their work. The lungs took in a great draft of air. And the Creator said, *"This man is alive, take off those bindings, there's life inside that mummy."* Death had been conquered by life.

We must realize that the unsaved man is dead toward God and all spiritual things. He is but a carcass wrapped tightly in the bindings of his own worldly desires and ambitions. He is earthbound in all his thoughts and appetites.

Only if we rightly diagnose man's disease will we prescribe the proper cure. Our own hearts tell us what the disease is; it is death and hostility toward God. We might despair if we didn't know by experience that there is a cure. If we could be raised from the dead so can others. But we must preach and prescribe for them the same medicine which healed our souls. If we needed a surgeon we must not prescribe an aspirin for others. If we needed resurrection we must preach resurrection. By our preaching we must command men to live. Our message must have the old Gospel in it; not the rubbed down and shiny cross that modern man wants, but the old rugged cross of shame. The one which speaks of the curse. But the only one which heals. The message which is foolishness to an intellectual and disappointing to the sign-seeker still is the power of God to those who trust it.

That sinner in your church does not need to listen to a finer choir or a more lively musical group. He does not need a more finely polished sermon. He doesn't need a more erudite preacher. He does not need a "testimony" from one of the world's elite. He doesn't need a psychological pep talk. He has been dead "four days and now stinks" and could not appreciate the best or worst in music or preaching. He needs the life-giving call of the Sovereign, *"Sinner, come forth."* He needs a miracle.

It has pleased the Father to provide just such miracles of His love and power when the message of the cross is preached to the spiritually dead. But it must be the cross that is preached. And it must be preached to men who are recognized as dead. But you will never preach it right unless you know

44

that you too were dead once but have been made alive by the sovereign grace of God. You will never believe in the miracle of spiritual resurrection like you will when you can look back and be honest about your own spiritual history. Your own personal experience will guarantee to you that God still brings the dead to life.

Then you will pray to God for the anointing which raises the dead. You will beg God for the Comforter to come and do what only God can do. Your preaching will become a resurrection call. And you will not be content with a superficial counting of decisions. Knowing that it is God who is giving the life you can wait for the genuine signs of life. And when you see that resurrected soul hungering and thirsting for more of the Word of God from week to week and from service to service you may then know that death is gone. The grave clothes have been removed. You will find what you expect to see in spiritual life: walking and leaping and praising God, not a half alive soul grunting along in the bindings of a mummy. And since that is the best that human effort can produce, you have to be content with it. The signs of real life can be expected when it is God who is doing the work. And if we believe that God is at work we can afford to wait for the complete birth to take place in those that He is calling to Himself.

To the man who believes in election by a sovereign God preaching becomes an activity of resurrection. Not the persuading of the human will to aid in its own salvation. Nor the appeal to a hostile heart to choose the God it disdains. But the declaring of the regenerating Word which marches into hell and commands that men live in the name of the Sovereign. "The gates of hell shall not prevail

Never say, "It doesn't matter,
It's only pitter-patter."

For you need strong meat,
With the devil to compete.

You're really no better than your diet.
Think not? Just try it.

For once in winning, Jesus said,
"You can't live alone by bread!"

45

CHAPTER SEVEN
HOW TO FIND THE ELECT

It is often charged that the doctine of election stifles the spirit of evangelism. It is claimed, and it has no doubt happened, that some church or missionary board has been frozen in their tracks by the doctrine. They have said, "It is not our work to save the heathen; when God is ready to save the elect He will do it by himself." So they sat and did nothing. And as a result the doctrine got a bad name. For it is assumed that the lethargy of such men is caused by their belief in election. But is this true? Is it the doctrine or the men who are to blame? Don't good men sometimes misuse right doctrine? Can it not be that hard-headed, indifferent men twist truth to their advantage?

Peter warns the Christian that some of the things Paul says are not only difficult to understand but destructive if misused (II Peter 3:15,16). But the fact that some men twist scriptural truth to their own destruction is not a valid reason for discarding true doctrine. The solution to the problem is to first find out what the truth really is, then to apply it with the aid of the Spirit of Truth. The Holy Spirit is the Author of the entire Word of God. If we are sensitive to Him He will not allow us to cancel out one truth with another. The Lord Jesus Christ commanded us to go into all the world and preach the Gospel to every creature. He also declared that "all that the Father giveth me shall come to me" (John 6:37a). One could argue from John 6:37 that the elect will be saved regardless of whether we go and preach or stay home and sew. Some have certainly taken that position. But that conclusion is wrong. It may be logical; but it is also carnal neglect. We must face squarely all the revealed truth of the Bible. We must believe that all the elect will surely come. But our faith in that fact must lead us to Go and Preach. The Great Commission is not to be voided by unconditional election.

It is the preaching of the free grace of God and the offer of "Whosoever will may come" which draws the elect to salvation. This may sound contradictory to some but the preacher should not be chided for insisting on this seeming paradox.

Spurgeon was charged with inconsistency for inviting all to be saved while he believed only the elect would come. His insightful answer to his critics was, "If God would have painted a yellow stripe on the backs of the elect I would go around lifting shirts. But since he didn't I must preach 'whosoever will' and when 'whosoever' believes I know he is one of the elect." Here is the true spiritual balance. It gives confidence to the preacher and is fair with the Word of God. And in the end it is the assurance the evangelist needs to stimulate him to greater effort.

To believe in election is not to disbelieve in hard work. It may be used by some as an excuse for their lethargy. But it has been a constant incentive for countless others. For belief in sovereign election promises much fruit without fail as a result of hard work. To believe it is to engage in labor with the certainty in the back of one's mind that God has indeed commissioned the work and therefore it cannot fail.

It is a matter of biblical record that the most arduous labors come out of faith in a sovereign God. A case in point is the ministry of the Apostle Paul. It is without doubt that he believed in unconditional election. If one is uncertain of this fact, read again chapter nine of Romans. Not once in all of the writings of Paul does he make God's choice of the elect dependent upon anything foreseen in them. His constant premise is that God's choice is controlled only by the "good pleasure of his own will" (Eph. 1:5). Moreover, it is the only possible conclusion to Luke's statement in Acts 13:48: "... and as many as were ordained to eternal life believed." We must assume that Paul would have agreed with Luke about this. For Luke could never have written what he did had it not also been the view of his apostolic leader. They must have agreed that election comes before faith and is the cause of it. It cannot be doubted that Paul believed and preached election. But did it cause him to be lazy? Was he indifferent to the Great Commission? Did he wait for "God" to save the heathen? Did he postpone preaching until the "chosen" came to him? Certainly not! Who labored harder? Who was more successful in planting churches? Who traveled more incessantly? Who endured more for the sake of the elect?

Paul believed in election and at the same time he had a heart full of compassion for the lost. He felt his heart stirred by the presence of the Spirit of Christ who came to seek and save the lost. That stirring led him to travel, suffer, write, and preach to reach the lost. And knowing that "all that the Father giveth shall come" his pace was quickened. The anticipated thrill of seeing them come allowed little rest.

The doctrine of election is not impractical. Nor is it a deterent to the hard work involved in evangelism. Paul told Timothy that knowledge of the

Inspired Word would equip men for all good works. Knowing the fact of sovereign election will equip a man for reaching the lost far more than teaching him any human method. For he will not only find a new hope of reaching the lost but he will be forced to depend upon God for guidance to find the elect. We may observe the Apostle Paul in his missionary work to learn how to find the chosen.

We find the Apostle Paul in the church at Antioch (Acts 13:1- 4). He is laboring in that great new Christian church. But in the back of his mind is the message given him by Ananias just three days after he was converted on the Damascus Road: "Paul, you are a chosen vessel, and you are going to bear the name of the Lord to the Gentiles, before Kings and the children of Israel." He was convinced that that was his calling! But how would it be carried out? Which direction should he take? Who should go with him? He could not preach to all the Gentiles in the Mediterranean world. How could he find the chosen? Where were they? What was the precise plan of God? At this point Paul teaches us a critical lesson. He shows us how faith in a sovereign God determines what steps to take when seeking to reach the lost. Paul's faith tells him that only God knows the ones he has chosen so he had better ask God for guidance to find them. Paul's faith tells him that only God can raise the spiritually dead to life. So he had better ask the blessing of God upon his efforts. He does not take a survey nor ask for suggestions from the church board. He prays. And he fasts. And he prays some more. And as he and his co-workers are ministering to the Lord, the Holy Ghost says, *"Separate me Barnabas and Saul for the work whereunto I have called them."* What an answer! What guidance! The church prays and lays hands upon them and sends them away. But Dr. Luke sees the real impetus behind the departure to the mission field. He says they departed to Seleucia *"Being sent forth by the Holy Ghost."* This was not man's plan. Man cannot find the elect. Man does not know whom to send. Man does not know where to go. Therefore Paul's first step was not planning but dependency. May it be ours!

The knowledge of the sovereignty of God in calling and election casts the preacher upon his knees to find the will of the sovereign. "Without me ye can do nothing," Jesus said. May we believe that enough to get upon our knees and plead with God for guidance and anointing to be *"Sent forth by the Holy Ghost."* We need to see our helplessness in this task of winning the lost. We need to see how desperately impotent we are without the Spirit of God. We would do well to say with Jehoshaphat, *"We do not know what to do, but our eyes are upon thee"* (II Chr. 20:12 RSV). Then we will hear from the Holy Ghost *"The battle is not yours but God's."* It was in a prayer room that the missionary labors of Paul were born. Knowing their need of sovereign help they pleaded it until it came. What prayers those must have been! Pleadings, arguments, prevailing supplications ascending up to the throne and returning with definite counsel and might. It will only be in such times that we find the mind of God for our tasks. Human planning and organization is essential. But it must be an effect not a cause of the Divine Blessing.

The agonizing of the local church body of believers will be answered by God's sovereign action. If we choose to scheme and plan on our own we may find ourselves to be armed only with our wits.

If we desire to win more souls we would do well to pray more. To submit all our plans to God. To see our helplessness. For without Him we cannot find the elect. Nor can we raise the dead. These things take supernatural guidance and resurrection power. And we have neither apart from Him. Let the local church pray earnestly. Let them beseech heaven, and the sovereign plan will unfold. The Holy Spirit will make known His commission. He will chart the course. He will seek and save the lost through us. And when He has thus spoken it will be our part to organize and go and preach. Then it will not be in our own strength. It will be the Life of the Vine flowing through the Branches. Jesus said this arrangement would bring forth much fruit. That is a promise that will work for any church which will bow its heart to the sovereign God.

The initial move toward winning the lost must be to seek the help of God. To get His guidance and anointing should be our first priority. We want to be "sent forth by the Holy Ghost." Then we can go and then we can preach. But where shall we go? To whom do we speak? Where are the elect and how do we find them? Is there sovereign guidance for this part of our task as well? Or does God send us out to guess and gamble?

We may look to Paul's second missionary journey to see how the God who calls also guides. We will see how the "steps of a righteous man are ordered by the Lord" whether he is seeking bread or souls.

Paul's second missionary trip takes him to revisit the churches he founded on his first journey. He travels through Syria, Cilicia, and Galatia confirming the churches. He delivers to them the decree ordained by the Jerusalem Council. As a result of the strength he imparts to them these churches increase in number daily. For the time being his work in these churches is done. He can now move on. But where shall he go? Which road shall he take? To which of the lost shall he next preach? He doesn't know. He has no direct line to God. He does not know the exact nature of the appointments God has scheduled for him. He does not know that Luke is waiting in Troas to become a member of his missionary company. He is not aware that Luke will someday write two major books of the New Testament. As a physician he will give to the world the most thoroughly researched account of the Virgin Birth and of the humanity of our Lord. As a historian he will record the critical days of the early church in the Book of Acts. Luke has been specially prepared by God for this work. This is an appointment Paul must keep. The apostle must be brought to Troas. Not just for Luke but for the sake of Europe and the western world. This is God's plan. Paul *must* get to Troas. For there he will receive a vision. A man will plead with him: *"Come over into Macedonia and help us."* That plea will pull him across the Bosporus Straits and salvation will have come to Europe and the peoples of the western world. But Paul is not privy to these plans. He can only take one step at a time and trust God to keep the appointments. His faith in a sovereign God assures him this will be. And God answers this faith.

Paul first decides to move toward Asia, the western section of modern Turkey. It is well populated and Paul no doubt felt it was a wise move. But that is not the way to Troas. So they *"were forbidden of the Holy Ghost to preach the word in Asia."* Paul then determines to go into Bithynia. *But the "spirit of Jesus did not allow them"* to go to Bithynia, for the sovereign God wants Paul in Troas and Troas is not in Bithynia. What other way can he move? Behind him are the churches he has just visited. On either side are areas which are forbidden to him at this point. The only path open is to the northwest. And so he arrived in Troas unaware that the Spirit has guided him to the porch of his most momentous days. From this day the history of Acts will be written from the standpoint of what *"We"* did, not what *"They"* did. The reader can notice for himself the change in the use of the pronoun *they* for *we*. Before Acts 16:8 Luke writes of the journeyings and preachings of others. And so he talks about what *they* did. But in Acts 16:10 he begins to record the activities of which he was a part. And so he says, *"we endeavored to go into Macedonia."* Paul has kept a pre-ordained appointment by simple trust in the "giver of all good and perfect gifts." He stands on the threshold of many miracles of grace simply because he submitted himself by prayer and faith to the Lord of the Harvest.

As we are "sent forth" by the Holy Ghost we will find the same sovereign guidance. The elect are in our communities. We can find them as we pray and go out trusting in the leading of the Spirit and the capability of Providence. An unbeliever will move next door to a real Christian and will find life. A change in working assignments in the shop will place an "empty" soul at the workbench of a "full" soul. Before long both will be full. A casual conversation at the hairdresser's boutique will result in a thirsty soul finding living water. Unaware of the power controlling him a high school counsellor will enroll a young lost girl in a class where she will sit at the desk with a praying Christian. She will find in that friend the Great Friend. Are these coincidences? Not in the opinion of faith. The Father is drawing to himself those whom he has chosen. And a share in the joy is promised to those who pray and lean upon the Spirit. Thereby the chosen in your community will be found.

It is the work of the Spirit of God to guide us to the elect. But of course that is not enough to save a lost soul. For having been found the chosen one must then hear the message. The Gospel must be preached. And even that is not sufficient. For a man cannot be converted unless he is given the ability to hear and understand.

When Paul reaches Philippi he learns of a place of worship down by the river. Women gather there for prayer. Among them is a woman named Lydia, from Thyatira, a city of Asia. She is a merchant of purple fabric. As a "worshipper of God" she listens as Paul preaches. Then she accepts the Christ whom Paul declares and is baptized. But how does Luke explain her conversion? Does he credit her with "seeking" out God? No. He says that God had to open her heart so that she could respond (Acts 16:14). Though she had come to a place of prayer she was bound by darkness. Even though she was a "worshipper of God" she was incapable of "seeing" the truth. Paul had been guided to her by the Spirit of God. He had been led to one of the elect by God. Then he had preached the truth to her. But a further work of "grace" is needed to bring her into the family of God. For she was incapable of responding to the Gospel until God pulled back the curtain of darkness from her eyes. And then she "attended unto the things which were spoken of Paul." The same Spirit who guided us *to* the elect will work *in* the elect to enable them to see and believe. Such miracles will be constant to the man preaching for the Sovereign God.

We may now make another observation about finding the elect. The finding and winning of the chosen is not subject to scientific analysis. It is not confined to a predictable pattern. The fisher of men never knows when his path will cross the one that God is calling. It will often be as he walks faithfully through the many different moods and vicissitudes of life that he will keep the divine appointments. Frequently it will be when he is in a providential prison that the fish will swim to the bait. Paul could never have encountered the Philippian jailer had it not been for the sovereignly arranged "stripes" and jail cell in Philippi. But Paul knew what to do with a jail cell. You sing in them. You praise God in them. And when the earth shakes the prison doors and when the keeper of the prison draws his sword to take his life you put the eager fish in the net. "Please, do yourself no harm. For we are not going anywhere." Paul might have added, "You are one of the elect and we were imprisoned to find you." But he didn't; he didn't have time. The Roman soldier fell to his knees and asked which way it was to heaven. And when this elect man finds that not only himself but his whole family will now go there he takes Paul and Silas to his own home and ministers to their wounds and feeds them. Paul has found a "chosen" household by being faithful to his God who puts him in prison to bring light to a soldier in darkness. The soldier saw a man who could sing in a prison and learns to sing the song of the free.

If you are eager to win souls you must answer God's Sovereignty with a life controlled by the Spirit of the Seeking Saviour. Let Him hold you in the "prison" of His choice if it means setting a prisoner free. He knows who is hungry for He has *"put it into their heart to come."* And they will come as you sing a song of grace in the trials and difficulties of life.

Sometimes, however, the burdens of seeking the elect are even too onerous for men like Paul. Then the Sovereign Comforter takes special measures. It was in Corinth that Paul needed the personal word from the One who called him to be an apostle before he was born and sent him forth in due time. His journey from Troas to Corinth had left him weak, fearful, and trembling (I Cor. 2:3). He had been dragged before the chief magistrates of Philippi by the owners of a demonized girl. They sought legal action against him when he exorcised the evil spirit which gave her the powers they found so profitable. And though Roman law prohibited the beating of a Roman citizen Paul was beaten with rods and fastened in the stocks. When it was discovered that he was a citizen of the empire the magistrates begged him to leave their city. He did so after encouraging the brethren gathered at Lydia's home.

He comes to Thessalonica and ministers to the Jews in their synagogue. He "reasons" with them from their Scriptures for three sabbaths. His labors bear fruit. While only a few Jews are converted, many God-fearing Greeks and "leading" women are won to faith in Christ. A new church is founded and begins to meet in the home of Jason. Seeing this success the unbelieving Jews become hostile. They conspire with wicked men to cause an uproar in the city. Jason is dragged before the now aroused authorities and is compelled to put up a bond to guarantee no further trouble. Because of their concern for Paul the brethren send him out of the melee to Berea. Paul's soul is thrilled in Berea. For he finds a synagogue anxious to hear the truth. Incessant searching of the Word leads many Jews and Greeks into the faith. But there is no time for a celebration. The hostile Jews of Thessalonica are approaching Berea to close the doors of the new church. Paul is again forced to flee.

He moves on to Athens, the epitome of Greek philosophy and culture. While he waits there for Silas and Timothy he preaches in the synagogue and the market place. His message is considered "moronic" by the Greek intellectuals. They tag him the "Idle Babbler" (Acts 17:18). And after he preaches a magnificent sermon to the sophisticates of the Areopagus he is sneered at: "How ridiculous," they say, "how can there be a resurrection from the dead?" Just a few believe here and Paul moves on to Corinth.

In Corinth, he finds friends, Aquila and Priscilla, and a home. He needs both. For he is weak and afraid. And his apostolic health is not improved by his ministry in the synagogue. His own brothers, the Jews, resist the gospel and blaspheme him. Now he is trembling. He fears reprisal. He considers discontinuing his preaching in Corinth. "Silas and Timothy are in Corinth now, they can help the new church." It is not his body which is weary, for he was able to make tents with Aquila and Priscilla (Acts 18:3). It was his spirit which was lagging. Beatings, imprisonment, being pursued relentlessly from town to town, and not knowing who was friend or foe was draining the fight from his soul. And now he is blasphemed by the brothers for whom he was willing to die to save (Romans 9:1, 2).

Paul needs comfort, and the Comforter comes on a night of weariness. *"Paul, I want to tell you something,"* the Lord said. *"Be not afraid, but speak, and hold not thy peace. For I am with thee, and no man shall set on thee to hurt thee: For I have much people in this city"* (Acts 18:9,10). These words expel the weariness from his spirit. They breathe new life into him. He can go on if there will be no personal harm. He becomes excited at the thought that the Lord has "Many people in the city." His mind walks through the dark and corrupt streets of Corinth. "Where do the elect live?" he muses. "I can't tell, but if the Lord says they are here, I shall stay and watch them come." It is a new man which rises in the morning. With new vitality he begins a preaching ministry in Corinth which will last for eighteen months.

The God who had sent Paul out to find the chosen had not forsaken him. God did not fail in the hour when Paul might have. He was sustained by the Everlasting Arms of the sovereign and compassionate Lord of the Harvest.

What Jesus said to Paul in Corinth he says to us: "I have many people in your city. The elect are living up and down these corrupt streets. The apartments, condominiums, and homes of your city are inhabited by those who are chosen of God. At this moment you cannot identify them. Not by their address. Not by their style of life or morality. Nor by their pursuit of truth. They seem dead to you. But I have put it into their heart to come; and they will. Just believe and be faithful. See your own helplessness and pray.

Let my Spirit guide you to Troas Street; some of the elect live there. You will find another in the jail on Philippi Avenue. They will drive you from that place but in fleeing you will run right into some more of the chosen on Thessalonica Boulevard; just stop at Jason's place. Again you will flee for your life but you will be extremely fruitful on Noble Place in Berea; don't miss it.

"The Athens Culture Apartments will be a severe test and not too productive. But I have there one sophisticate, Dionysius, and one woman, Damaris, and a couple of others I want to bring into the fold. So drop by there and preach my Word. Don't worry about the 'name-calling;' I've given you a new name. Be strong in the Corinth Condominiums. It's a wicked place. But those rooms hold many that will live in my house forever. And I assure you, the manager, Gallio, won't bother you. Be strong now. Don't hold back the message. I will be with you in all of these places. Together we will find my elect. *All that the Father giveth shall come to me through you.*"

A vision of horror cast a gloom upon my mind.
I saw a man who wanted life of a different kind.
He was dark of skin and dark of thought.
He searched in vain for the eternal plot.

He was riding in a chariot along a desert road.
But he was drawn to a book as if by a goad.
He had been to worship at the city of peace,
But his heart said, "You have not found release."

So as the horses raced he felt a compelling
To find an answer in the prophet's telling.
"Of a lamb, silent and sheared," the prophet spoke.
"Humiliated, judged, cut off by a stroke."

He sensed that here was light which could set him free.
But the words were not clear and he said, "I pray thee,
Someone...please tell me of the prophet's cries...
Does he speak of himself? Who is it that dies?"

The gloom that I felt was for this man's plea.
I knew only Jesus could make him see.
For a moment I thought a terrible thing.
He would return to his queen and never...never...sing.

What he required was a man with blessed feet,
Who would interpret the book and sit in his seat.
One who would tell him of Jesus who died.
A man like Philip who was proven and tried.

Who when the Spirit speaks does not refuse
To go to whomever God might choose.
Philip came and unto the man Jesus preached.
And into a dark, searching soul God reached.

There was no doubt that the answer had been found,
For when water was seen the eunuch jumped to the ground.
"Philip," he said, "Please bury me there,
For in the Christ you preach I have found my share."

CHAPTER EIGHT
HOW TO RECOGNIZE THE ELECT!

Is it possible for men to tell who are elect? Are there definite and reliable signs present in the chosen of God? How do the elect respond when they hear the preaching of the Gospel? These are important considerations. For the preaching of the Grace of God usually calls forth several types of reactions. Several of these reactions appear to be valid. But the appearance may be superficial. Jesus put His finger on this issue when He told the Parable of the Soils in Matthew 13. Of the four types of soil, one was incapable of accepting the seed. But three of the four did accept the seed and produced life; however, only one of these three was genuine. In the end the good soil alone produced plants which continued to show the evidences of life. The leaves were bright. The stalks were tall and straight. They constantly grew. And they produced a usable fruit. Life was evident.

Among the many responses to the preaching of the Word only that of the elect is genuine and capable of bearing fruit unto God. Only the elect have the good soil which will accept the seed of the Word and produce a new creature. What are the signs of this good soil? How does soil prepared by God respond to the seed of God's Gospel? How do the elect respond to preaching so that we can know that they are indeed elect? What should we look for in those who respond to altar calls and decision times? And what should we anticipate seeing in the lives of those who come forward for Christ which will give us assurance that they are among the chosen of God?

In I Thessalonians the Apostle Paul gives us the signs which will help us recognize the elect. Consider verses 4-7 of chapter One.

> Knowing, brethren beloved, your election of God. For our gospel came not unto you in word only, but also in power, and in the Holy Ghost, and in much assurance: As ye know what manner of men we were among you for your sake. And ye became followers of us, and of the Lord, having received the word in much affliction, with joy of the Holy Ghost: so that ye were ensamples to all that believe in Macedonia and Achaia.

These verses describe the response of the Thessalonians to the Gospel message Paul preached to them on his second missionary journey. And these signs indicated to Paul that they were chosen of God. For in verse four he says, *"knowing...your election of God."* He was certain that they were chosen; he *knew* it. How did he know it? Verses five through seven explain it. He knew it because of the way the Gospel came to them. Let us consider these signs of election.

The first thing Paul saw which indicated their election was the *absence of indifference.* He says, *"For our gospel came not unto you in word only."* The Thessalonians did not treat the Gospel as mere words. It was not meaningless to them. It was not foolishness like it was to the men on Mars Hill who thought it to be speculation. "Nonsense," they cried. They pooh-poohed it. And that is exactly the reaction of those who hear the Gospel but do not have a "heart" to come. It simply has no appeal to them. They can hear the "Old, old story of Love and Grace" and be unmoved and unresponsive. It is just so many words. Their minds are preoccupied. Their hearts are already committed. They think only of their next meal or game or moment of pleasure. The present rate of inflation or recession is the topic which dominates their waking moments. Their next weekend trip or the coming "sports classic" is their worldly prize. So the "Hill of the Skull" smothered with the darkness of "forsakenness" doesn't interest them. It has no bearing upon their current pleasure. The Son of Man, the willing Lamb, pierced and bleeding, has no value to them. If they desired to they could "Look and Live." But they would rather just live without looking. "Let me focus on myself; Let me live life my way," they protest. And so the seed falls upon the hard path and the birds come and find a meal. Satan has snatched the Bread of Life from another soul. But that soul will not know it until it will be too late to *Look* and *Live*. When it could have mattered the Gospel was only a bunch of words.

But the Gospel affects the elect in a far different way. It comes to them in *power*. They are gripped by it. They cannot get away from it. Their minds are seized by the words. Their hearts are drawn. They can think of little else. The Cross pulls them, for they see now how a holy God can save them. He has atoned for their transgressions. The Crucified Saviour is attractive to them. They are pulled by the loveliness of His Grace. They are compelled by the preaching. Their hearts burn within them as regenerating forces renew their dead spirit. "Chords that were broken vibrate once more." The message is not just words to them; it is Bread for the hungry.

There are also positive indications that the Holy Spirit of God is working upon the heart when the Gospel is preached to the elect. It is evident as you observe the elect man that there is a heavenly power regenerating his personality. The man who used to "yawn" all the way through the sermon now sits in absorbed attention. He now has "ears to hear." Worship which was once a waste of time is now enthralling. What is the difference? It's the same church, the same preacher and the same Gospel. But God has made him alive. The "renewing of the Holy Ghost" has given a deep yearning for the things of God. Every time you open the church doors he will be there. The Holy Ghost, the Helper, will see to that. And if he does not come through those open doors we may well wonder if he is truly born of God. If there is no deepening hunger for the Word of the Father we may well question the sonship. For when the Holy Spirit comes into the heart of the elect he makes that child zealous for the honor of the Father. *"Because the love of God (for God) is shed abroad in our hearts by the Holy Ghost which is given unto us."*

Furthermore, the chosen man *receives the Word of God with deep assurance.* He does not treat it as some curious philosophy. He is convinced that it is true. He may not comprehend all of the particulars but he is certain that the message is from God. This assurance is more than the power of logic or intellectual persuasion. It is the seal of truth stamped upon the heart of the elect man by the Holy Spirit. "He has received an anointing by which he knows" (I John 2:20). As an elect man he was already "doing" truth (John 3:21). And when he heard the gospel of truth he was aroused. It had already been put into his heart to come. Something deep inside him made him desire the message he was hearing. And when he heard it the deepest desires of his awakening spirit were answered. With an instinct born of God the assurance compelled him to faith.

This faith begins to move his life in a new direction. When the Thessalonians believed they began to follow Paul and his message. Their assurance made them disciples. And true conversion will make men disciples today, not just curious about doctrine, nor skeptical believers who are always learning but never "knowing." The elect come to personal awareness of truth and reality. They hear the gospel and drop their nets. They answer the call, "Follow me." They follow their spiritual fathers in the faith. They follow the Lord of their spiritual fathers, and the elect continue to follow even when it means affliction. For the elect are convinced they are in the way of life wherever it might lead them.

Being so convinced they see in their troubles reliable evidence of their place in God's family. They see their difficulties as a share in the sufferings of Christ. And they recognize that all those who have become fit for the fellowship of heaven will have trouble in this present evil age. Knowing all this they have the "joy of the Holy Ghost." And this joy makes them rousing examples to other believers.

These are the evidences of election Paul saw in the Thessalonians. And just such signs we can expect in those elect people who respond to our preaching. Moreover, we must not be satisfied without seeing these manifestations of life. We must demand them before we accept the genuineness of conversions. The "decisions" we observe should always make us rejoice. But we must not be naive. Many of these conversions are spurious. They may show some of the expected signs of real spiritual life but as time moves along it will become clear that they do not have eternal life. It takes time to demonstrate the validity of real conversions.

Jesus was making this clear to us in the Parable of the Soils (Matthew 13). Life sprang from three of the four types of soils. The shallow rocky ground produced life. The weed-infested soil produced life. And much life and fruit were produced by the good soil. And so it appeared at the onset that all three of these soils were good. But from the very moment of sowing two of the three were incapable of sustaining life. This was not evident at the time of sowing. Nor was it visible in the early days of the life of the plants. All three soils produced plant-life which might have appeared of equal size and quality when it was two weeks out of the ground. They might have each received an equally good prognosis. It might have appeared that all three would endure and produce much fruit. But with the heat of the sun the life in the shallow ground withered. With the competing weeds and thorns the life in the weedy ground was choked out. Only the remaining good ground continued to produce life and fruit.

Among our converts there are those with good heartsoil. They have hearts prepared by God. And when they hear the gospel life springs forth. Time and testing will prove the genuineness of their spiritual life.

There are others who respond who do not have good heart-soil. Life appears to be there, but with the coming of persecution and the competition of worldly ambitions the superficial life is choked out.

We must be aware of this superficial character of many conversions. We must not give our full approval to any man who "walks the aisle" before we see in him true signs of election. To accept a man as a real Christian before we see the evidences of life is to encourage that man in a false hope. If God is converting the heart then we can expect the convert to rise up and walk in a new way. If he does not live a new life but continues to show interest we must preach and pray until the full work is done. For it may be that the saving work is only beginning. Full birth and full fruit may only be forthcoming after a deeper work of the Spirit of God. During the time this work takes we must not stand aloof from this brother. We must love him.

We must treat him warmly. But we must not be content until we see the biblical evidences of divine election.

If such wariness seems unjustified we may remind ourselves that it is nothing less than what Jesus showed in His dealings with new believers. John tells us that when Jesus was in Jerusalem for the Passover, "many believed in His name" (John 2:13-25). They had been impressed by His miracles. They gave him allegiance. But Jesus was not impressed with their commitment. And, therefore, He did not make a commitment to them. John explains our Lord's reluctance by saying, *"For He knew all men, and because He did not need anyone to bear witness concerning man for He himself knew what was in man."* Jesus was wary of the fickleness of man. He was suspicious of the religious instincts of the natural man. He knew human impulsiveness. He knew the natural heart of man is impressed and attracted by supernatural displays of power. He knew that man can make a commitment from this impression without his heart and spirit being affected. An undiscerning mind may begin and end a commitment with equal ease. Jesus knew better than to accept this "belief" at face value.

It must not be thought, however, that Jesus was not ready to divulge himself to anyone at that moment. The dialogue with Nicodemus proves otherwise. John 3:1 clearly places Nicodemus in contrast to the superficial believers of John 2:23-25. In the RSV the reading of John 3:1 is *"Now there was a man of the Pharisees, named Nicodemus...."* The *"now"* can also be translated *"but."* And this gives the proper sense of the verse. John is contrasting Nicodemus with those believers to whom Jesus would not commit Himself. John is saying, *"But there was a man of the Pharisees, named Nicodemus..."* to whom Jesus could and did commit Himself. Jesus was ready to manifest Himself when He found genuine interest and faith. But He was suspicious of much "faith." For He knew what was in man.

The same "seeing-through" man is seen in John 6. A great multitude of "followers" traipse behind Jesus at the Sea of Galilee. They are absorbed with His miracles. By an awesome display of power He feeds five thousand men from five loaves and two fishes. The people are terribly impressed. They proclaim *"This is of a truth the prophet that should come into the world."* They intended to make Him king. But was Jesus impressed with their proclamation? Did He go along with their proposal? Does He trust their discipleship? No. For instead of commending He rebukes them. *"Truly, truly, I say to you, you seek me not because you saw signs, but because you did eat of the loaves, and were filled."* Their discipleship came from their stomachs not from their hearts. Our Lord's miracles were

60

"signs" of His deity. But they were blind to this fact. They were moved only by their physical hunger and possibly, their curiosity.

We have the same type of response today. The church is attractive to many people for purely natural reasons. Some like the beautiful music of the Christians for its settling and comforting effect. They are inspired by it. It reminds them of a happy childhood. It satisfies their basic religious instinct to worship. But in reality there is no spiritual motivation or awareness present. It is only a vicarious participation in the valid worship of the truly redeemed.

Others find the atmosphere of love and fellowship in the church to be a welcome haven. They cuddle up in it as in a warm womb. Though they have no faith they like to associate with those who do. It is comforting to them to have such an environment.

There are those who are deeply enamored with anyone who purports to have a special calling or gift from the Spirit of God. Some of those "believers" have a compelling, but blind allegiance to their cherished "charismatic." Often these people are unable to find God on their own. In their insecurity they seek for some demonstration or proof of the Spirit's presence in the electrifying atmosphere of "healing" meetings and "charismatic" circles. That is not to say that God does not heal or work in the charismatic groups, nor that believers do not need inspiration and emotional experiences. But it is to recognize the high emotional charge of those meetings, and to recognize that emotional sensations can often make a weak faith appear strong, even when real knowledge and faith is most tenuous. It seems wrong that their loyalty is accepted by so many as unquestionable faith. It has been my experience that this faith is extremely perishable. Often it meets with utter ruin at the hands of the common reverses of life. And many times it refuses to accept the leadership of godly men who teach the Word of God. It is simply preoccupied with the miraculous. Peculiar focus! And one wonders if it is saving faith in the Lord or merely idle seeking after welfare bread.

On the surface it appears that all of these superficial "believers" are following Jesus Christ. But would Jesus commit himself to them? Or would He treat them with the same caution we find in John's gospel?

There are two significant questions which must be asked about these people. First, what will happen to them when times of testing come? And second, are they capable of facing the facts of spiritual life? The "disciples" of Jesus were turned off by the spiritual truth He gave them. They simply stopped following Him (John 6:65). Why did they stop? Let us consider some reasons. Firstly, we must notice that Jesus had put His finger on their

61

real motivation (John 6:26). He let them see that they were really following not Him but their stomachs. He burst their religious pretenses. Secondly, He made it quite clear that His real work had to do with spiritual life. He had not come to feed the world. He had come to feed the spiritually hungry. He told them He was the Bread of Life. And if they would eat of Him they would never hunger again (John 6:35). He told them that they could not have life unless they ate His flesh and drank His blood (John 6:53). They may not have understood completely His meaning, but they knew He had spoken directly against their basic desires. They were repulsed by His message. It had no place in their thinking for they were but natural men. Thirdly, He made it obvious that He thought that human life on the natural level (without the Spirit) was unprofitable. "The flesh profiteth nothing." He told them that his words were "spirit and life" and they could only be received by those who were being drawn by the Father (John 6:44,65). These pseudo-disciples could only come up with one opinion of Jesus' words: they were "hard sayings" (John 6:60). Their expression more properly described their own hearts. They had been faced with eternal, saving truth and had been unwilling to accept it. The truth was made known to them and they withdrew into darkness. For John tells us that from this time *"many of his disciples went back and walked no more with him."* In masses they had followed Him for miracles of bread. But now the facts of spiritual life had repelled them. Their motives had been wrong from the beginning and Jesus had known it. That was why He had given them the discourse on the Bread of Life. That was why He had told them that it was not the human will which makes a man come to God (John 1:12,13) but the drawing of the Father's will. *"Only the spirit can give life."* So in spite of the appearance of real discipleship and faith they fell back when their motives were tested. Their faith, at least at this point is spurious. There may come a time when they will return to the truth for worthy reasons. But for now they must not be considered among the "chosen." For the chosen manifest both a love for the truth and an endurance amidst difficulty (I Thess.1).

Would we not be doing well to show a little more of the "caution" demonstrated by the Lord of the Harvest? We might do it just for love's sake; to be a little more suspicious of the reality of conversions until we see the genuine signs of election. We might then avoid some of the frustrations of having to mold the feebly converted into usable instruments of grace. If we would only wait on the full work of God we might find that God really can convert the soul into a new man. Or we might also find that with the preaching of truth and the presence of trouble the "hailed" convert will prove deficient.

Of course, it is not ours to make the final judgment concerning the salvation of men. But with the presence of divinely inspired evidences we cannot go wrong by testing our work to see if it bears the hallmark of the Spirit. Apparently Paul did so.

There may be and are many reasons for the original interest a human being shows in the gospel of Jesus Christ. The inspired music of joyful hearts may be the first thing to touch the soul of the unsaved man. The warmth of the "communion of the saints" will most certainly penetrate many in this lonely world. The touch of miracle will always incite men to interest and faith. We would leave out none of the ways by which God first approaches a soul. May all of these "signs" point more men to Life. But once having entered the path the decision must be tested to see if the momentum is just the push of a sign or the pull of God. If it is merely the excitement of the natural heart of fallen man who feels good being religious the path will prove rough, and retreat will follow. But if it's the pull of the Sovereign God who "put it into the heart to come" that soul will continue on that road. And though it prove slippery and he fall "he will not be utterly cast down, for he delighteth in his way" (Ps. 37:27).

I know you are chosen
From the way you act.
Your faith in Him
Is indeed a fact.

It is not your experiment
To try for a while,
And when it doesn't pay
Shrug it off with a smile.

No, to you it is real,
A pearl of great price.
You arise when you fall,
And you do.....once or twice.

I see in you
An assurance and power.
The Gospel put it in you
In that very first hour.

By the Spirit you have
Found the elect's one addiction,
God is to be loved and praised
In spite of affliction.

The signs are clear,
Plentiful in reflection.
I rejoice with you,
Knowing your election.

CHAPTER NINE
JESUS AND ELECTION

The normal human response to the doctrine of divine unconditional election is amazing to behold. Of all the teachings of Holy Scripture it seems to be the one which elicits the most antagonism from man. It must be due to the very nature of the sinful heart of man. And this is true whether the man is a believer or an unbeliever. The unsaved man, being in darkness, naturally thinks of God as dependent upon man. It is his opinion that God chooses only those who choose Him. But many believers are of the same opinion and show equal consternation at the thought of God being sovereign in electing some of mankind to be saved. It would appear that the same "enmity" toward God can motivate the saved as well as the lost. When we remember the place where we got this hostile mind within us we can see the reason. In the Garden the great issue was *"Who shall govern? Who shall have ultimate control? Shall the creature or the creator be submissive? Shall the divine program be adopted or shall man try his own plan?"* Scripture reveals that man tried his own ways. He chose independence. He wanted to be left alone. He decided to exalt himself. He would achieve true life on his own. And in doing so he made a god out of himself. He would follow his natural drives. He would listen to his own voice first. And above all he would maintain his own sovereignty. This was the heart man had when he walked out of the garden. And this is the heart man has today. A heart that never leaves him even when he is born again. A set of the mind which seeks to impose his own will and sovereignty upon all it touches. A bent of the soul which can only be overcome in the believer by the indwelling life of the Lord Jesus Christ. For only the power of the resurrected and risen Lord can turn the saved man from his own sovereignty.

It should not surprise us then that man, whether Christian or not, reacts with hostility toward the teaching of the sovereignty of God in election. For no other doctrine approaches the saved man with such insistence upon surrender. The believer finds the doctrine of salvation by grace a welcome relief to his own feeling of lostness and demerit. He welcomes it. The promise of the presence of the Spirit is enjoyed for the strength and healing it brings. The believer rejoices in the knowledge of the Coming Christ. All of these are wonderful advantages to him. But when he faces the thought of the sovereign God he often feels that he has reached the point where compliance has no benefit to him. He is being asked to give up both his view of his own supposed sovereignty and his belief that though lost he was capable of choosing God. This is painful. The proud human spirit fights this truth. In the Garden the clay determined to control the Potter. It said, *"I will make of myself what I want to make of myself."* And even in the Christian these words find an echo as man retorts to God, *"You can only make me what I allow you to make of me; you may save me, but it will only be with my permission."* Every atom of the human spirit rejects the idea of being "mere clay." It would rather be clay with fifty-one percent of the potter's stock. Just a "mere" controlling interest. And even the one who believes solidly in the sovereignty of God finds a peculiar satisfaction in leaving God with forty-nine percent of the firm.

This antagonism aroused by the doctrine of election is not to be charged to "controversial" preachers who dare to believe the truth of God's Word. The Word must be accepted as it is even if some of man's cherished ideas are controverted. The real antagonism is due to the human heart. It is the direct result of the conflict which stems from that enmity the human heart feels for its Maker.

This enmity was often in focus in the ministry of the Lord Jesus. At the very beginning of his ministry it was the thought of divine election which aroused the hostility of the people of Nazareth (Luke 4:16-32). He had gone into their synagogue on the Sabbath day to read the scriptures. He read from Isaiah:

> The spirit of the Lord is upon me, because he hath anointed me to preach the gospel to the poor; he hath sent me to heal the brokenhearted, to preach deliverance to the captives, and the recovery of sight to the blind, to set at liberty them that are bruised, to preach the acceptable year of the Lord.

When he had finished the people's eyes were glued to him. He answered their stare by saying, *"This day is this scripture fulfilled in your ears."* They wondered who he was and seemed to seek a sign. But Jesus saw their unbelief. He rejected their desire for "proof." Instead, He said to them, *"No prophet is accepted in his own country."* Then He did something which made them hate Him and seek to destroy Him. He said that while there were many widows in the days of Elijah during the famine the prophet was sent to only one of them. He added that while there were many lepers in the times of Elisha only Naaman received the healing grace of God. The implication was clear. Their hearts, filled with rejection and unbelief, were convulsed at the thought of being passed by. *"Could this man, the mere son of a carpenter, be saying that we are not chosen? Could he be intimating that we have no automatic claim as Jews to the full blessing of God?"* Indeed He was and they knew it. They were *"filled with wrath, and rose up, and thrust him out of the city, and led him unto the brow of the hill whereon their city was built, that they might cast him headlong. But he passing through the midst of them went his way."* Interesting, isn't it, what the thought of a sovereign God will do to the thinking of the human race?

Man was infected in the Garden with a disease which will not leave him. The fever may be quieted at times but the germ remains. It will not be eradicated until "death is swallowed up in victory." May that final cure come, quickly! As long as man is man his natural will must be set against the divine will. It is clear from Scripture (Rom. 8:7) that the "carnal mind is emnity against God." What else can we expect then from the natural and carnal man but hostility when the truth is presented? What can we expect from the natural man in the use of his own will but rejection when faced with the Gospel of the God he resents?

This is where we must solve the issue of the freedom of man's will. Does man ever use his own will to choose God? Does the human will save the soul? Certainly not if we are to take the witness of the Bible. Again we may look to the words of Jesus to see the direction the human will takes.

It is now toward the end of Jesus' earthly life. He has entered Jerusalem ready to face the Cross. He is preaching to the crowds at the temple and He utters the lamentable cry, "O Jerusalem, Jerusalem, thou that killest the prophets, and stonest them which are sent unto thee, how often would I have gathered thy children together, even as a hen gathereth her chickens under her wings, and ye would not!" (Matt. 23:37). Has more pathos ever been put into language? Jesus stands yearning for the city to come to Him. The divine will was to gather the people together and shelter them. To teach them. To mother them. To save them. But where lay the fault? Why did not the "meeting" take place? *Ye would not! Ye would not!* The human will would not move toward God. Man stood in the presence of the Saviour and he *would not* be saved. He felt the touch of God and he *would not* touch back. He heard the words of life but he *would not* listen. Is it not true that the human will never saves? The human will only condemns and damns. The free will of man is always used to move against the love of God in spite of the most merciful appeals. *"I would...but ye would not."*

Is this not the picture of the world as it hears the gospel? They are told that it is a message of grace, unmerited favor; *"You who are in prison are free. The ransom has been paid. All you have to do is walk out the door. See, the door is open; Jesus opened it. Just leave your cells and come out into liberty and life. When you leave your cell God will take you by the hand and make a new life for you under His blessing. He will gather you under His wings and give you abundant shelter and care. He will place you into His family and treat you like a son though you aren't worthy to be even a servant. He will write your name in Heaven's book and though you die before the final days of history you will not be forgotten. He will remember you and give you room in the special place He is preparing for eternal living. And, of course, all of this is free of cost to you. So why don't you come out of prison into life? O soul, please come."* But do they come? No, for they prefer their own way. They are in the prisons of their own desires. They are incarcerated by their own ambitions. They are chained by the desires of the flesh and of the mind. They are captives of this world. They don't see or care for the next.

So, then, if man does not respond to the loving appeals of God, why do we then charge God with injustice for allowing man to live on in His preferred rebellion? And why then should we have any reaction but adoration for the fact that out of these rebels God chooses some to receive His grace? In choosing some He has done nothing but let the others have their way. And even then He is extremely patient toward those who fit themselves for destruction (Rom. 9:22, 23). Rightly understood, Scriptures show God to *be perfectly righteous in rejection, and completely free in election.* Furthermore, it magnifies the grace of God to see that it is from the ungodly and the "foolish" of the world that He draws His own (I Cor. 1:26-31).

When we see that the gospel call goes out to all it will help us discern what Jesus meant when He said, *"many are called but few are chosen"* (Matt. 20:16 and 22:14). For the invitation of the gospel does indeed go out to all and is sincerely extended to the whole world. But with unanimity it is rejected. So then in the sovereignty of God some are chosen out of the world to be made willing to come. May God be praised that He saves any of the sons of Adam. Moreover, we may be certain that those who have been chosen will come. Our Lord said, *"All that the Father giveth me shall come to me, and him that cometh to me I shall in no wise cast out"* (John 6:37). The elect are sure to come. It never occurred to Paul or Jesus that somehow the chosen of God could be missed. They knew that as they walked according to the will and timing of the Spirit of God they would find the elect and that the elect would respond to the Word. This must have been a dominating influence upon their thinking as they moved from village to town to city. It must have exerted a regulating effect upon their minds as they sought to "seek and save the lost." For while both Jesus and Paul were always working we do not see frenzy in their labors. They are not frantic in their preaching. They are possessed with a feeling of "divine timing" in all that they do. This is demonstrated most clearly in the ministry of our Lord.

Notice the pace which Jesus followed. The consciousness of sovereign timing in His ministry. When pressed by His mother to manifest Himself He would say *"Mine hour is not yet come."* Yet this did not deter Him from prosecuting the present call and tasks of His service to men. So while He would not fully divulge Himself to those in Cana of Galilee He did manifest His glory by providing wine for the wedding feast. He would do what the occasion needed but He would not hurry the sovereign plan.

All the time He worked and traveled He was conscious of the "plan" being fulfilled. Even the accidents of His physical needs were instruments in its out-working. Moving toward Galilee to escape the clamoring crowds (John 4:1f.) He becomes weary as He travels through Samaria. Needing rest He sat down beside Jacob's well. He is alone for the disciples have gone to the city to buy food. And in this perfect moment of time, His aloneness at the well and the disciples absence to buy food, a woman appears. Only such a one as Jesus could meet her soul's need. Weariness along a chosen path has caused Him to pause for the meeting. Her need is such that a private talk is required. Providence had sent the disciples from the counseling room. In that room she finds living water; she drinks and shows the fountain to her city. Many more come and drink. There are no accidents or coincidences here. The journey to Galilee, the precise arrival at the well, the weariness which forced a rest, the coming of the "thirsty" one at the right moment; no, these are not accidents, but sovereign love in action.

A sovereignty which works among us too. How often salvation comes to a home when a Christian moves next door. Accidental purchase? No. The escrow was processed by heaven. The title was searched by God. No one else on earth could occupy that house! What about the friend that you met at school? The one who made the Lord lovely to you. Why you? Why the chance meeting? So much, even eternal life, turned on those moments. There might have been so many slip-ups; but there weren't any, were there? The steps of a righteous man are ordered by the Lord even before he knows it.

May we not have the same confidence as we walk according to the will of God? May we not be certain that we will cross the paths of the elect? Can we

69

not believe that the divine appointments will be kept? Can we not teach all believers to be on the lookout during the prosecution of our normal duties of life for "thirsty ones"? That is clearly the implication of the Word of God, *"All that the Father giveth will come."* While we rest, conduct our business, converse with neighbors, and keep social engagements the elect come. Tired of the broad road they will join our company on the narrow but certain road to the celestial city. They will be irresistibly drawn to the fellowship of the Light, for they prefer light. They will love us for they have begun to love God. The truth we speak will be to them a regenerating power. They will drink deeply and go to tell others.

All of this will be accomplished without frenzy or the use of frantic measures. It will not be the uptight believer who will meet the elect. He will be too busy trying to manufacture conversions and "experiences" to be aware of true thirst. It will more likely be the calm and trusting fisherman who will feel the slight nibble of the catchable fish. He will realize that he is dealing with a great prize. Not a trophy to be forced to its knees in praise of the fisherman's ploys; but a delicate and fragile human heart. Handle with care! A new creation is taking place inside that sinful skin. One of Adam's race is joining the family of God. See your impotency, O soul-winner. At best you are an instrument of the divine hand. Tenderly love that soul as it emerges from the womb. Don't put it through your denominational paces. Don't make a Pharisee of it. Gently clear its eyes with the silver nitrate of grace. Remove the impediments to breathing with care of love. Wrap it warmly in the fellowship of manly sainthood. Constant guarding and warm milk will make a strong son of God. There is no place here for frenzy. No room for noise or nervousness. Let the baby rest. God's babies always survive. We can count on that. It cost God too much for His family to let even one slip away.

Across your path
From day to day,
Come the elect
To hear you say.

Oh, friend of mine,
God loves you so.
Jesus gave His life
This love to show.

I see in your eye
A deep strong yearning,
To find the *real* life
And spiritual learning.

So do not wait,
Come to Him now.
That's it.....trust him,
Before Him bow.

We did not just happen
To meet in this place.
God arranged it so
You could see His face.

For it is true,
"all that He giveth shall come."
Even to the least and last
Of His elect sum."

CHAPTER TEN
RECONCILIATION OR COMPATIBILITY?

To introduce the thoughts of this chapter let me quote from a biography of Charles Haddon Spurgeon by his close friend, W. Y. Fullerton.

> Preaching in Leeds for the Baptist Union in a Methodist Chapel on a memorable occasion, he read the tenth chapter of Romans. Pausing at the thirteenth verse, he remarked, *"Dear me, how wonderfully like John Wesley the apostle talked.* 'Whosoever shall call.' *Whosoever.* Why, that is a Methodist word, is it not?"
>
> "Glory! Glory! Hallelujah!" came the response.
>
> "Yes, dear brothers," the preacher added, "but read the ninth chapter of the epistle, and see how wonderfully like John Calvin he talked—'That the purpose of God according to election might stand.'"
>
> Smiles on the faces of those that had before been silent were the only response to this utterance. "The fact is," continued the preacher, "that the whole of truth is neither here nor there, neither in this system nor in that, neither with this man nor that. Be it ours to know what is scriptural in all systems and to receive it."

Is it not our aim to know and preach what is scriptural? Indeed that should be our highest goal! Might we not know more of the fruitfulness of the Prince of Preachers if we were willing to strike all of the notes of the gospel message? Do we not hamper our efforts by dwelling only on our denominational bias? Those who see only the sovereignty of God in the Bible often become indifferent toward the world. Those who see only man's responsibility so soon become oriented toward psychological cures and tend to be sentimental toward man's condition. They seem to be possessed with a sickly pity over man's so-called weaknesses. "What a shame," they say, "that man is caught in this trap of sin." They forget that man made his own trap. Then he fell into it. He is responsible for his own predicament. Is there not a way to avoid being caught in either camp of narrowness where we preach only part of the truth?

In this chapter I would like to offer some thoughts concerning the proper means of handling the paradoxes we find when we study the subject of the sovereignty of God. They are not new ideas. They are simply the fruit of much reflection upon our duty toward the teachings of the Word of God. In the process I will comment upon some of the objections frequently raised about unconditional election.

The first concept which draws our attention is the proper method of handling truths which seem to contradict each other. The obvious problem before us is that of how to harmonize, if possible, the truth of the sovereignty of God with the truth of human freedom and responsibility. It seems to me that this is the point where men most often go astray when considering the doctrine of election. The honest student is cognizant of the fact that the Word of God teaches the sovereignty of God. (In that concept must be placed the fact of God's unconditional election of men to salvation.) The fact of God's overlordship is patent to any student of the Word of God. He cannot look at the Psalms, Isaiah, Romans 8,9, Ephesians 1 and the Book of Revelation, not to mention all of the others, without knowing God is Master. He is also aware that the Bible holds man responsible for his own sins and salvation. By turning to God man may be saved. The offer is to "whosoever will" and the price is paid.

The student who knows these complementing truths now has a choice to make. The decision he makes at this point will determine whether he stays within the biblical framework or whether he looks to human reason for his final answer. If he decides to seek a middle ground between the sovereignty of God and the freedom of man he will find himself leaning upon human reason to interpret the mind of God. If he decides to let the two seemingly contradictory truths stand in his mind as a paradox and believe both, he will find himself upon the happy ground of divine inspiration instead of finite aspiration. He is happy who lets God be the final arbiter.

But not all men feel this way. Having found the paradox they cannot rest until they have married the irreconcilable parties. They feel that they must improve upon the divine method of Holy Writ. Are they justified in this move? Is it right to let the human mind construct a concept which is not adequately based in the Bible? Does man have a right to force his own conclusions upon the Bible when those positions do indeed change the substance of divine revelation?

Let us look at the issue by following a man as he learns from the Bible the truths of the sovereignty of God, including election, and the responsibility of man. *His Bible study brings to him the truth of the unconditional sovereignty of God.* This concept can definitely be traced to the Word of

73

God. Yes, God is sovereign and is accountable to no one for his actions. He does all things well and his only rule is that he "worketh all things after the counsel of his own will" (Eph. 1:11; also 1:5,9).

This concept can be diagrammed this way so as to see its basis in the Bible:

Next, the student sees the truth of human responsibility. This concept too can be traced to the Word of God. Man is responsible. His own decision determines his destiny. *This concept can be seen in this way for it is rooted in the Word of God.*

Now the Bible student has arrived at the critical juncture. He must decide what to do with these two opposing truths. He can do one of two things.

1. *He can let them stand as he has learned them, parallel and irreconcilable,* in which case the diagram would appear this way:

If he does this he is on solid biblical ground. For the Bible definitely teaches both of those truths. If he does not do this then he can take the alternative.

2. *He can attempt to reconcile the two opposing concepts by human reason and produce a third concept unsupportable by the Word of God.* In this option the reasoning will go something like this:

"I know God is sovereign.

"I know that man is free.

"But these two thoughts contradict each other so there must be some middle ground where they come together.

75

"It must be, therefore, that God in his sovereignty decides to save the man who in his freedom chooses God.

"Yes, that is the way to harmonize these truths. 'Man chooses God and then God chooses that man.' "

The diagram would then look like this:

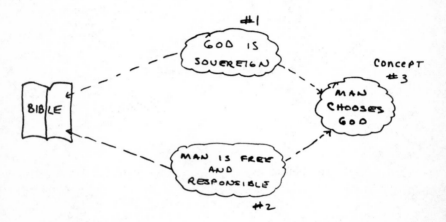

The important thing to recognize at this point is that in the attempt to harmonize concept #1 with concept #2 we have developed a third concept. Furthermore, we must point out that concept #3 is based on human reason. It cannot be found in the Word of God. If it is not supplied by human reason it simply would not exist for the pages of Holy Scripture are void of it. The diagram would then look like this:

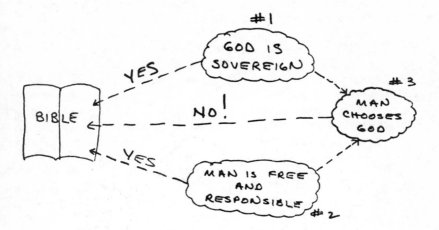

The essential issue before us is whether or not man has the right to construct concept #3. Can man supply by dint of human reason a concept not found in the Bible? Is it not dangerous handling of the Word of God to "add" a human thought to the divine thoughts? Especially when it deteriorates substantially the concept of the sovereignty of God by making him almost dependent upon man? Does it not take away from God by adding to man?

Why don't we just let the Word of God stand on its own? If God did not try to satisfy human reason why should we? Why should we who believe that the Bible is the only standard of truth be put in the position of trying to improve upon it by human means? What do we want: human wisdom or the wisdom of God? Shall man's wisdom seek to "add or subtract" from the divine store? Shall we compromise the biblical truth of unconditional election by making it conditional upon human choice? Shall we deny the biblical truth of human "hostility" toward God by saying that man is capable of choosing God? *"God forbid; Yea, let God be true, but every man a liar "* (Rom. 3:4 a).

Let us lay aside human reasoning to discover the truth of God's electing grace. Human wisdom could not devise the wonderful plan of redemption (I Cor. 1:17-21). And human reason is equally poor in interpreting divine redemption. Let us not try to appease our logical faculty by tainting the truth which satisfies our needy souls. We are to live "by every word which proceeds out of the mouth of God." It seems to me that the Word is fit for us in the very form in which it comes from the mouth of God and does not need to be "processed" by human reason.

Let us turn our attention to another problem which arises in our minds concerning unconditional election. How can it ever be said by God *"Jacob have I loved, Esau have I hated"*? Is that not an atrocious thought? How could God hate Esau? Is that not unrighteous? But do we not make a large mistake here? It is a miscalculation which makes us focus our attention more upon God's just treatment of Esau than upon God's graciousness toward Jacob. We must not forget that neither Jacob nor Esau merited in any way the divine love and mercy. That God could hate Esau was perfectly just. Esau deserved nor desired nothing different. But that God should love Jacob was testimony only to the immense love of God. We are all too often found guilty of sentimentalism. Thinking ourselves to be deserving we think that somehow Esau was treated unkindly; that maybe he was really a deserving man who got lost in the busy courts of heaven. The same sentimentalism which wants to discount hell and blame God for all human suffering, sides with Esau and forgets the glory of God in loving Jacob. A woman came to Charles Spurgeon once and said that she had a problem with the statement, *"Esau have I hated. How could God hate Esau?"* Mr. Spurgeon's answer was, *"That's not my problem, lady; my problem is how could God love Jacob?"* And that should be our amazement too. That God could hate Esau is understandable. For Esau despised everything God had done for him. He resisted the divine goodness and grace. He disdained God. Of course, Jacob was hardly better, which only highlights the love of God.

"That God could love a sinner such as I," how wonderful is love like this.

The wonder of wonders is that God could and did love any of the sons of Adam. Why did He not just destroy the whole race and start over? Why should He love any Jacob? Why did He not hate all? Who of us did not deserve the "end" of Esau? Who feels superior to him? Yet God has loved us while we were as undeserving. May God be praised!

Then there is the suspicion that belief in unconditional election shuts off compassion. It is thought that no man will have true compassion for the lost if he believes that the elect and only the elect will come, and that, furthermore, they are certain to come. But in reality it does not seem to work that way. For greater compassion has not been seen than in men who have believed thoroughly in divine election. George Whitefield was a thorough believer in unconditional election and no one could argue with his evangelistic efforts born of love and compassion for the lost world. In

1739 he began preaching in the open air to coal-miners in Bristol. He met with great success. He urged John Wesley to try the same method. Whitefield once preached to something close to thirty-thousand people at once in Boston. Kenneth Scott Latourette, in his book, *A History of Christianity,* tells us that the Great Awakening was powerfully reinforced by George Whitefield (1714-1770). His great work did not come from a compassionless heart.

Who would argue with the love and mercifulness of Charles Haddon Spurgeon? Listen to his words:

> Love is the true way of soul winning, for when I spoke of storming the walls, and when I spoke of wrestling, these were but metaphors, but this is near the fact. We win by love. We win hearts for Jesus by love; by sympathy with their sorrow; by anxiety lest they should perish; by pleading with God for them with all our hearts that they should not be left to die unsaved; by pleading with them for God that, for their own sake, they would seek mercy and find grace *(The Soul Winner, p. 112).*

> Soul-saving requires a heart that beats hard against the ribs. It requires a soul full of the milk of human kindness; this is the *sine qua non* of success (p. 113).

His compassion was no more meager than his success. And yet he believed unconditional election to be the biblical doctrine that it is.

The Apostle Paul comes to our mind as a further example. Intriguing as it is, it is in the same chapter where he writes of election that he opens his compassionate heart for all to see. Romans 9:1-3:

> *I say the truth in Christ, I lie not, my conscience also bearing me witness in the Holy Ghost, that I have great heaviness and continual sorrow in my heart. For I could wish that myself were accursed from Christ for my Brethren, my kinsmen according to the flesh.*

He certainly was not lying; neither when he spoke of election nor when he lets us feel his heart. His labors demonstrate his love to be genuine, his compassion real. I do not know how the man who believes in election comes by such great compassion, but it seems to be there. It may be that since he feels so loved by unconditional love which sought him and bought him that compassion readily flows to those in need. He may feel a debtor; he has freely received and he freely gives. In God's Family, to be greatly loved is to want to love. Or it might be that he loves because he has partaken

79

of the very nature and life of God by His Spirit. It is the nature of God to love and that nature and its instincts are communicated to the man who is born of God. Or it may be that this man loves for both of these reasons plus others. But let the charge not be laid against the doctrine of election that it shuts off human compassion. Let the record show that that is the abnormal exception rather than the rule for those born of God and not by the will of man. Faith in sovereign election and compassion for the lost have always gone and will continue to go any lengths to save souls.

Consider Luke's picture of Jesus as he stands outside Jerusalem. Luke 9:51 to 19:44 has been called the Great Insertion. The gospel writer follows Jesus for ten chapters as He moves from Galilee to the Cross. The Lord has "set his face to go to Jerusalem." He knows what awaits. He knows the opposition. He is cognizant of the contradiction of sinners. And He journeys to Jerusalem willing to face the consequences of human sin. Seven times in these chapters Luke mentions that Jesus is traveling inexorably toward Jerusalem (9:51; 13:22; 17:11; 18:31; 19:11, 28, 37). During this trip He gives the great stories of the New Testament: The Prodigal Son and the Loving Father, The Good Samaritan and His gracious care, the publican beating upon his breast, the salvation of Zaccheus. All of these stories speak of His love and compassion to the lost. And then when He arrives at the city, Luke says: *"And when He was come near, He beheld the city, and wept over it, saying, if thou hadst known, even thou, at least in this thy day, the things which belong unto thy peace! But now they are hid from thine eyes."* That Jesus taught election is unquestionable. But that in His perfect manhood there was compassion is obvious throughout the gospels. And here He stands as God in the flesh and weeps over the lost city. Sovereignty and love come from the same fount. We are made strong by the sovereignty; and we are made usable by the love. Those who truly partake of the Spirit of their Lord will weep with their weeping God at the sight of this lost world.

And these tears will be more than superficial emotions; they will be the throb of the soul. Hosea felt the yearnings of God's love when he wrote for God: *"How shall I give thee up, Ephraim? How shall I deliver thee, Israel? How shall I make thee as Zeboim? Mine heart is turned within me, my repentings are kindled together"* (Hosea 11:8).

The man who is the friend of the sovereign God will also feel within himself the love of his Sovereign. He may not do it from the same perspective as his Lord but his Lord's words may find expression in that man's prayers over his own city.

Oh, City, City, how often I would have brought you together with your God, and Saviour. I would have met you anywhere at your convenience. I would have come to your home. I would have met you in your schools and halls. I would have spoken to you at any length in the stores or on the streets. I would have lovingly told you of God and Heaven. I could have brought healing to your heart and your home. I could have given you peace and assurance. It would have been yours without price or cost. But you would not. You were busy with your religious dress. You were preoccupied with your own ways. You were caught up in having fun. And now summer is gone and you are not saved.

Sovereignty does not shut out love. Neither Jehovah nor his ministers are impassive toward the lost. Their hearts break and yearn with deep emotion for a world which seeks first its own. Only election can save it. But it is a wrong use of election which cancels compassion.

I would like to suggest as the last point of this chapter that the paradoxical truths of the sovereignty of God and the freedom of man have more than just a parallel relationship to each other. In the work of the ministry they seem also to be sequential in the experience of preaching to win and equip man.

In preaching to persuade the unbeliever we do not begin by declaring divine election. We begin by presenting the good news of God's love and Christ's atonement. We point to the convicting law and the wages of sin. We endeavor to speak those things which can be used by the Spirit of Truth to convict that lost man of his need of faith in Christ. And the Holy Spirit honors our work by convincing men of truth. In many cases men are so deeply persuaded of their lostness and the justice of their condemnation that they almost despair of approaching God. It is then that we must sound the message of "Whosoever will may come." No man is disqualified or ineligible because of his sins or his demerit. "Whosoever is athirst, let him come and take of the water of life freely." "The Spirit and the Bride say 'come.' " "Him that cometh to me I will in no wise cast out." The seeking, hungering, thirsty sinner must be made to see that all he needs is to come. The only prerequisite is to Look and Live. He need bring nothing in his hand. No sacrifice or offering with which to pay the price. The cost has been borne by his Saviour. And thus the door is open to any and all who come in simple faith. Men would despair of salvation if they could not see written above the door: *Whosoever will may come.* All are welcomed. God can accept anyone. God has justly dealt with all sin (Rom. 3:26) and therefore he can justify the most ungodly. Let no hungry soul have fear of approaching the throne of Grace. *"Whosoever believeth shall not be ashamed."*

As he looked at the door of salvation from the outside he saw the free invitation: *Whosoever will may come."* Encouraged by the generous offer he enters. And when he turns to look back at the point of entry he reads, *"Chosen before the foundation of the world."* He asks, "What does that mean?" The biblical answer comes to him: "God chose you and made you willing to come through the door. You were living in willful hostility toward Him but He loved you with an everlasting love and drew you to Himself." The new believer is filled with awe as the Holy Spirit witnesses to him that the God he had offended loved him and healed him. He has no words to utter his praise. But his heart is filled with love and thankfulness. His will be a life worthy of God. For he has tasted of a love far beyond human dimensions. *"Herein is love, not that we loved God, but that He loved us, and sent His son to be the propitiation for our sins. Beloved, if God so loved us, we ought to love one another."*

"Whosoever will" was the love that pulled him through the door. The love of the "Divine Elector" made him never want to leave. "You can't find love like this behind just any door."

SAMSON THE FUTILE

So you're good at riddles, you can
reconcile all of the divine paradoxes.
You have caught the loose ends and
tied their tails together like foxes.

So what do you have in your complex system
of humanly devised smoke and fire?
You burned the field, drove the foxes insane,
applauded yourself, and gave your hair for hire.

CHAPTER ELEVEN
WHAT IS TO BE GAINED?

In this book I have addressed what I think to be a most serious problem. Namely, that the doctrine of unconditional election is not given its proper biblical emphasis in the pulpits of today. In some cases it is ignored; election is never mentioned. In others it is sidestepped by an appeal to philosophy or human reason. It is suggested that God would not want us to be content with the paradox involved in believing in the sovereignty of God and preaching the responsibility of man. Therefore, we must do something with the apparent contradiction of these truths. And so some middle ground is adopted which seriously compromises the biblical position.

I have tried to show what the proper stance is for those who want to be fair with the Word of God. I have demonstrated that to accept a set of truths which are parallel to each other and leave them that way is not unwise. It is the better part of wisdom to speak only where God speaks and not to speak where He has remained silent.

I have also attempted to bring forth certain implications of the doctrine of election; for example, its significance to evangelism, to humility, to courage in service, to understanding man. These have been discussed within the biblical framework. We have found that it is a most practical truth.

As I have written, however, many other relevant thoughts have come to mind. But to keep from being overly long they will be put into one final chapter.

In this last chapter let us ask the simple question, *"What is to be gained?"* And we will answer it by saying that there is much, very much, to be gained by a careful consideration of and belief in the doctrine of unconditional election.

First of all, there is the satisfaction of soul to be found in being completely open to all of the Word of God.

For one reason or another most of us Christians have prejudices against some or several of the truths of the Word of God. Perish the thought that there might ever be such a thing as a "denominational bias," but it has been known to exist in remote regions. Most of us find the Lord in some kind of denominational setting. And we are seen looking at the Word of God through filters issued to us at denominational headquarters. We are assured that "it is for our best. We want to guard you from all kinds of potential evil in the doctrines of others." And with that most of us are content.

But somewhere along the path of our lives in the Lord we begin to wonder if the church is really as infallible as it pretends to be. This is a good moment. For it can be the moment when a soul comes out of trusting second-hand truth, masticated and spoon-fed to us by those who feel that their bias is also God's, to an honest look into the Word of God. It can mark the awakening of a soul when it says: *"Let's just see if God can hold His own against the denominational platform. I'm going back to the Bible. I'm going to exercise my Reformation right to let the Word of God be the final court of appeal."* It might not be a bad thing for more of us to start wondering: *"That if the denomination says it and the Bible doesn't something is wrong with the denomination. If the Bible says it and the denomination doesn't, something needs to be done."* A word of caution here: this is not a plea for revolution or uprising, but one for prayer and burden. The truth will not be established by the disjointing of tempers or brothers. But the truth must be established. If the Bible says it, every Christian should know it and every preacher should preach it. That some won't should not deter us.

I have found in the experience of coming to know divine election an extreme satisfaction, one whch is born of the knowledge that I have found the truth. I have found a truth beyond which I cannot go. I am forced to rest in God. *"He says it, I believe it."* The matter has been settled by the highest court. And there it stands.

I entered into battle with God. My opinion against His. My thoughts seeking to leave their imprint upon His. My mind trying to make God act like man would. I tried this and I lost. God's Word would not let me win. His ways were higher than my ways. And in the surrender, I found a joy and a peace well worth the loss of pride and self-esteem. There is a "divine glow" that fills the heart when we find ourselves aligned with the Word of God without vacillation. It is comforting to know that if we just let God do the talking we will not be guilty of false preaching. If we only speak what is written, interpreted with sound principles of hermeneutics, we cannot but speak truth and in the end set men free.

The false prophet is one who imposes his own view upon the Word of

God. He can't quite let God have the final say. Usually he is not totally wrong in his views. He may even be right in most of them. But real honesty eludes him because his own ideas and feelings are so strong. In commenting upon the false prophets of Ezekiel's time, H. L. Ellison says,

> Instead of letting themselves be dominated by the Spirit of God, they were dominated by their own desires and motives. It is not the worldly or "unsound" teacher or preacher who is the real danger to the church, but the man who allows himself to be dominated so by his own deepest desires that he is preaching them, although he has convinced himself that it is the Word of God he is preaching.

Having come to the place where God has won a major victory over my own deepest feelings by being convinced that a doctrine which I once rejected is true, I find much desire to check myself constantly on all points of my preaching. I discover a deep yearning to be honest with all of God's Word so that I might speak as the "oracles of God."

I have also come to the place where I do not worry about the message, for it does not originate with me. If I am rightly interpreting the Bible, then the message is from God and not from me. He stands behind it and by it He will bring forth fruit.

Whatever you might have to concede to arrive at the truth, it will be worth it. I cannot agree that we must hold on to our beginning biases for the sake of unity and tradition. There is nothing holy about a denominational prejudice which does not have roots in Holy Scripture. It is not "untouchable." Concede what you must, much or little, but be honest with the Gospel of the Grace of God. All you have to gain is the truth and the joy of being aligned with God. You may start your own "reformation."

A second benefit to be found is the wonderful enhancement of the view of God which is afforded us as we come to believe in election.

We discover that there is a real God. The Almighty does indeed exist. Far above all principalities and powers of heaven and hell there lives one who is absolute in His Lordship. He seeks counsel from no one. He seeks no advice. He is utterly self-sufficient. He is the eternal *I am*. And He is accountable to no creature. We cannot call Him into question. He does not submit His proposals to either angelic congress or human inquiry. He does what He wants according to the advice of His own immutable and perfect character.

To believe this is to be made aware that indeed the universe has a sovereign. To accept this doctrine is to realize that we have a God, one who is worthy of the Name. At the feet of such a sovereign we will humbly bow.

We will be thankful to be not His counselor but His children. *What greatness in the Father! What blessedness in the children!*

We also have in the doctrine of unconditional election a deeper appreciation of the love of God.

No true Christian doubts that God loves him. But the amount of love he feels will be largely determined by his view of how and when God's love came to him. If he feels that God's *choice* of him was conditional, depending upon his choice of God, he may also feel that God's *Love* is conditional. Love may be to him the result of a contract offered by God: "I will love you first," He says, "And if you will love me in return I will then love you even more."

But if he believes that God has loved him with an everlasting love and therefore he chose Him and called Him, the sense of love is far deeper. For now we have love that was in full bloom before the reconciliation took place. We have love that was not dependent upon a "deal." We have here love unqualified, unconditional and overwhelming. It is awesome and inexhaustible in its dimensions.

This love is further magnified to know that it was not a love just aimed vaguely at the whole world but that we were loved by name before the world began. It was specific. He loved us according to our own identity and uniqueness of personality at a time prior to our knowledge or acceptance of Him.

What we have to gain here is a feeling of identity so virile as to drown the "identity" crisis. Ordinarily men may wonder who they are and why they are here. We cannot share their dilemma. We know. For we have been loved by God. There has never been an instant in the history of the universe or of the Trinity of God when we were not known as we are. We always were and always will be in His heart and mind.

We may also consider empowerment for service and prayer as a gain to be found in election.

Why are we engaged in divine service and ministry to men? Is it not because we have been placed there by God? And does God fail in any enterprise? Does not revelation inform us that we were "chosen to go and bring forth fruit?" If that is true can we not then plead God's purpose as a reason for Him to answer our prayers.

My Father in Heaven, it is your work in me that makes me want to bear fruit, to see souls saved and the people of God revived and filled with your presence. This is not my program, O God, it is yours. These desires are not natural to me. They must come from you. Will you not then honor the ambitions of your own Spirit who lives within me?

Grant the success that you have made me ask for. Make me as fruitful as you intended me to be. Let not your work fail. Let me fulfill all that you planned to do with my life. Amen.

If God chose us and called us before the world began then we can plead that very purpose in our prayers. *"Let not one word of your plan fail, Father. Let it be done to me and through my ministry exactly as you planned. Let me finish my course."* It will surely happen.

I cannot help but believe that many of the deep spiritual yearnings which arise within our hearts are nothing but the hints of His predestinated plans. And if we will honor these suggestions the plans will blossom into full fruit. Pray about your spiritual desires until God either removes them or answers them. We must believe that while God has ordained great things to happen to us it is by our prayers that they will occur. Spurgeon put it this way "...our prayers are in the predestination, and that God has as much ordained His people's prayers as anything else, and when we pray we are producing links in the chain of ordained facts. Destiny decrees that I should pray—I pray; destiny decress that I shall be answered, and the answer comes to me."

Realize that your prayers are but "links in the chain of ordained facts." See your prayer as a connection between the predestination of God and the actual working out of great things. Honor the Spirit of God within you and pray for the things He lays upon your heart. If it is a holy and proper desire, it has come from the Father's counsel and will be granted to you as you plead His purposes.

Pray for more souls to be saved for that is God's revealed purpose. Pray for more biblical religion for God has indeed given us only one revelation of Himself. Pray for more spiritual life in your people for that is God's prime intent for His redeemed. Pray for an increase in your church and that God would set before you an "open door." Pray for an increase in the power of your preaching for it is God's revealed purpose to save people through preaching. Pray for a better understanding of the Word, for your people can only "live by every word that proceeds out of the mouth of God." Pray for yourself for God has paid a great price to give you abundance of life. These benefits are ours by God's grace. They are rooted in the Word of God and will find the consent of the Spirit of God within us. By having faith in God's predestinating power, we will find prayer to be a way to get things done.

Not only will election greatly help our prayers, but it will significantly increase our vision for our service to men. We will be more able to withstand the "failing hearts" and "fainting spells" which attempt to subdue us. We will be able to endure the failures and disappointments which are part of ministry, for "If God be for us, who can be against us?"

It will guide us to believe that our later years can be more useful and productive than our apprenticeship. Andrew Blackwood, the Professor of Homiletics at Princeton Theological Seminary, once said, "Plan to do your best work after fifty." That is good counsel. But how do we last until fifty? And of those who do last how many arrive at this age spent and worn? Assuredly, much of the toil and weariness is natural to the work of God. And it is to be appreciated in those who have so arduously labored. But is not also much of the strain in our nerves and emotions? Is it not true that much of the burden we feel is due to the fact that we try to carry what is not ours to carry? Without a sovereign, who, apart from our counsel and help, ordains, sets up, pulls down, and saves? We try to be responsible for too much. We accept responsibility for what God alone can do and we become exhausted trying to accomplish the impossible in our own power. Moses was eighty when his great work commenced. When he was dying at one hundred and twenty neither his sight nor his vigor were impaired. Certainly this was the exception but even here we can learn, for can it not be said that the source of Moses' vitality was that meeting with and recognition of the *Great* I AM at the burning bush? And in finding the real God, Moses knew that not himself but God carried the burden. His part was to trust and follow and lean upon God by prayer, but not to create or generate things by his own power. May we not also find a significant improvement in physical and mental outlook if we were to take the long look and see ourselves fulfilling the purposes of God formulated in eternity and certain of success if prosecuted by a man confessedly impotent in ability but confident in his God.

Election can help us purify and make worthy our methods of evangelism.

Everyone will have his own ideas and criterion here but it is something which needs to be discussed. Can we be honest with the Old Rugged Cross and still try to embellish it with modern methods of communication and entertainment? Does the Cross have more power when presented by a "converted" celebrity? Does rock music make the Gospel more acceptable to youth? Do we have to speak the language of our hearers to genuinely communicate with them? Certainly we want to be clear, plain, and capable of speaking in the language of the common man. But do we have to use all of the vulgarisms and slang of the schoolyard to preach our message of reconciliation? How much must we adapt to our hearers preferences in style of music and identification with "personalities?" We cannot recommend the banishment of any method. But do we not need to look at the Cross as the power of God and realize that anything we do to enhance it is in the end taking away from the designated plan of God? It is the preaching of the Cross that saves the lost. God's wisdom is bound up in it. It is His glory. If Jesus declared that *"All that the Father giveth me shall come to me,"* and the Bible makes it plain that it is the preaching of the Gospel that is the power of God unto salvation, ought we not to make sovereignty our trust and the cross our message? All other matters are incidental. Music should be good but it is not the essential matter. The "testimonies" of dramatic conversion are often inspiring but of how much real significance in the spiritual work of God is a matter open to debate. The use of people with "names" is good promotion but it is something which Paul would caution us about (I Cor. 1:11-31;3:1-23). The Gospel does not become more believable just because some popular personality has decided to throw in his lot. It is only the Spirit of God which can draw the human heart and when He does the faith will stand in the power of God and not in the wisdom of men. Let's give the world what they need; simple statements of biblical truth. Let the emphasis always be upon the crucified Christ. Let no "emotional experience," baptism, or second work of grace ever detract from the central place of the Cross and we will see souls saved. When the cross is kept in the center all of the other truths will find their proper orbit. The cross is the "power of God" and we have the word of the Sovereign on that. And now one final word.

The goal of this book is not to coax anyone into idle speculation about the sovereignty of God. Rather, it is to declare an unquestionable biblical truth. That the truth of unconditional election be known by every believer in Christ is my prayer. But not merely for the sake of adding another doctrine to their supply do they need to know. In the end all truth is practical. We do indeed *"Live by every word that comes out of the mouth of God."* And so I see two practical ways in which belief in election will aid the average believer in his daily life. First, it will give him much assurance and faith in his God and in his personal salvation. This is a much needed experience in our insecure age. And secondly, the believer will be much better prepared for service in winning souls when he sees himself as sovereignly guided by the predestined plan of God to cross the path of the elect. To do great things we need to know our Great God.

Remember the former things of old: For I am God, and there is none else: I am God, and there is none like me, declaring the end from the beginning, and from ancient times the things that are not yet done,

saying, my counsel shall stand, and I shall do all my pleasure....I have
spoken it, I will also bring it to pass; I have purposed it, I will also do it.
(Isa. 46:9-11)

What is your need, friend?
Souls?
Power?
Prayers?
Poise?
Destiny?

Where have you looked, friend?
Reason?
Man's Subtle schemes?
Your mind?

Why not look to God, Unsearchable riches!
Higher ways!
Higher thoughts!
Predestined paths!
Eternal roots!
He is Lord.
And He fills all.

THE AUTHOR

The Rev. Kenneth D. Johns has pastored the Trinity Bible Chapel in Rowland Heights, California for the past fifteen years. He is a graduate of Life Bible College.

A native of California he lives in Rowland Heights with his wife and three children.

BIBLIOGRAPHY

Stifler, James M., *THE EPISTLE TO THE ROMANS,* Fleming H. Revell Company, New York, London, 1897. The quotations found in Chapter 2 on Page 9 and 10 are taken from Mr. Stifler's book, pages 172 and 173.

Strong, James, *THE EXHAUSTIVE CONCORDANCE OF THE BIBLE,* Abingdon Press, New York, Nashville, 1890. The various meanings of "Foreknowledge" as written about in this book, Chapter 3, Page 20, were taken from Mr. Strong's concordance.

Moule, Handley, C. G., *THE EPISTLE TO THE ROMANS,* Pickering & Inglis Ltd. London. A quotation is taken from Moule's writings (p. 237) and appears on Page 20 of Chapter 3.

Godet, F., *COMMENTARY ON THE EPISTLE TO THE ROMANS,* Zondervan Publishing Company, 1883, 1956. Mr. Godet's view of election is Arminian. But the translators have included in their appendix two excellent notes on the proper view of *Foreordination* (p.523), and *Freedom and Sovereignty* (p. 525f.). The direct quotation of Cremer is taken from pages 524, 525. These appendices are extremely valuable and appear in Chapter 3, Page 20.

THE INTERNATIONAL STANDARD BIBLE ENCYCLOPEDIA, General Editor, James Orr, Wm. B. Eerdmans Publishing Co., Grand Rapids, Michigan, 1943. Volume II, page 1130 provides a discussion of the word "Foreknowledge" which I have used in Chapter 3, Page 21.

Tenney, Merril C., *NEW TESTAMENT SURVEY,* Wm. B. Eerdmans Publishing Co., Grand Rapids, Michigan, 1961. Mr. Tenney provides a probable date for John's Gospel (p. 189) and is referred to in Chapter 4, Page 27.

Latourette, Kenneth Scott, *A HISTORY OF CHRISTIANITY,* Harper and Brothers, New York, 1953. Page 959 provides the historical setting for the reference contained in Chapter 10, Page 78 and 79.

Ellison, H. L., *EZEKIEL: THE MAN AND HIS MESSAGE,* Wm. B. Eerdmans Publishing Co., 1956. Page 55 of Mr. Ellison's book provides a quotation used in Chapter 11, Page 85.

The references to and quotation of Charles Spurgeon come from three books:

Fuller, David Otis (condensed and edited by) *THE SOUL WINNER,* Zondervan Publishing House, Grand Rapids, Michigan, 1948.

Spurgeon, C. H., *TWELVE SERMONS ON PRAYER,* Baker Book House, Grand Rapids, Michigan, 1971.

Fullerton, W. T., *CHARLES HADDON SPURGEON,* Moody Press, Chicago, 1920, 1966.